The Decisive Woman

The
DECISIVE WOMAN

Marion Duckworth

VICTOR BOOKS
A DIVISION OF SCRIPTURE PRESS PUBLICATIONS INC.
USA CANADA ENGLAND

Copyediting: Barbara Williams
Cover Design: Paul Higdon

Library of Congress Cataloging-in-Publication Data

Duckworth, Marion.
    The decisive woman / Marion Duckworth.
      p.   cm.
    ISBN 1-56476-058-8
    1. Women, Christian—Conduct of life. 2. Decision-making (Ethics) I. Title.
    BJ1610.D83   1993
    248.8'43—dc20   92-42638
                                      CIP

*To my husband John, who
contributed significantly to these pages
and who has always encouraged
me to think for myself*

and

*Thanks to those dedicated
Christian scholars who have gone
before. Some of your names I've
mentioned in this book.
Your ministry to me has
been invaluable.*

Contents

Letter to the Reader

If writing a book is like being pregnant, as many writers say, then my pregnancy has been a very long one. An elephant could have gestated in less time because from idea to finished manuscript it has taken seven years.

That's because, in the beginning, I wasn't decisive enough to write *The Decisive Woman*. When first asked, "Why write a book directed only to women on the subject of making moral choices?" I didn't know how to answer. I know now.

We female humans need such a book because of our unique position and role in society and because we live in an era with more moral choices peculiar to us than any era before it.

This book doesn't tell you *what* to think. God doesn't do so in areas of nonabsolutes, so why should I? It does tell you *how* to think — how to determine what's right for you in these sticky areas of life.

If you're like I am, you want to be reasonably sure a book is going to help you in some significant way before you spend money on it. Even though *The Decisive Woman* doesn't provide answers tied in neat bundles to tuck in your psyche, it does provide exactly the kind of help you do need to deal with the moral issues that make your spirits sink and your blood pressures soar.

If you pursue the process described in this book, besides knowing how to decide...

whether or not to side with your grandmother who wants to refuse chemotherapy for her cancer...

whether or not to vote for the best-qualified candidate even though his views on abortion are different from yours...

something else will happen.

You'll find yourself becoming a more confident Christian woman. That's what the process has done for me.

Yours in the love of God,

Marion Duckworth

The Choices We Face

ONE ❧

*T*he retreat was held in a new, Hilton-like resort hotel overlooking the golf course. I wasn't fooled, however, by the luxurious indoor pool, the thick pile carpets, or even by my two-room, posh suite. In spite of the fact that I had two television sets, a bouquet of flowers, a private dressing room with a thick, terrycloth robe hanging in the closet, everything was not "right."

As a retreat speaker, I'd been invited to camps in the woods with bathrooms down the hall or even out-of-doors. On one retreat grounds, my cabin was heated with a glowing wood stove and my bed covered with a handmade quilt. In another, there was *only* a bed; no dresser, no chair, no table and, of course, no clothes hangers. Why provide clothes hangers when there was no closet to hang them in?

The amenities never mattered to me. Only the women

mattered. And everywhere they were the same. On Friday evenings at the beginning of the retreat they were bright-eyed and chattering like teens at a pajama party. I'd overhear whispers to put birdseed in Diana's sleeping bag or to hide Cindy's clothes. Sprinkled among the women were the quiet ones, munching chips and cookies, smiling and wondering aloud if they'd be able to get any sleep.

As I rode down in the new elevator to the new meeting room in the new hotel on Friday evening, I thought of Saturday morning. Yawning from talking half the night and desperate for a cup of coffee, the women would drift into the meeting room again for the first session of the day. They'd giggle and squeal over the previous night's antics: singing Christmas carols to the speaker at midnight (even though it was April); playing Pictionary until 2 A.M.

By midmorning, however, the bright-eyed, first-day-in-Disneyland look would fade. Carefully applied, best-self layers would fall away. That's when I'd make my offer again. "If you have something on your mind you need to talk about, please come see me."

They'd come. Confused, because they had questions to which they didn't know how to find answers. I certainly knew how they felt. Once upon a time, I too had been confused and pressed down by my own questions to which I didn't know how to find answers.

THE RIGHT THING TO DO

After that retreat, a fortyish brunette came to the front after I finished speaking. I led her back to my room. "I just found out that my son is homosexual. He's living with his lover in another state."

Her smile cracked, and then her voice. "I don't know how

to treat him. I feel sick inside when I think of the two of them together. The baby boy that I nursed and rocked and walked the floor with. My husband and I are going to be taking a trip, and we'll be in his city. Do we go to his house? Stay with them? I don't know what the right thing to do is."

In a Western state I sat on the grass under the big sky with a troubled brunette who twisted a strand of her hair as she talked. "My husband abuses me." Her voice was flat, as though she were ordering a burger and cola in a fast-food restaurant. "The kids have seen him do it. My mother says I should get a divorce, but she's not a Christian. Afterward, he says he's sorry and I feel as though I should forgive him. Isn't that the Christian thing to do?"

In the Midwest, I sat on the sofa in my motel-like room with a stylishly thin and stylishly dressed woman who'd been one of the quiet ones on Friday evening, disappearing for bed early. "My teenage daughter is sleeping with her boyfriend. We've tried everything to keep them apart, tried to talk with her, but nothing works. Should I see that she gets birth control pills so she doesn't get pregnant? Is that right? Or is it compromising with sin?"

At a retreat center near my own city, I answered a knock on the door of my room on the campgrounds at bedtime. "The other day I stopped by and picked up my four-year-old grandson and took him to the park. When I helped him go to the bathroom, I found out that his buttocks were black and blue. My daughter's been abusing him. She's a single parent and is having trouble dealing with that. I've seen her in action with Davie, and I know what happens when she loses her temper. What do I do? Report her to the authorities? I've talked with her, asked her to get help, but she won't even admit she has a problem."

After the retreats, we pack up our curling irons and Bibles and go home. The troubled women to whom I spoke, and those to whom I didn't because they were too afraid to open up, go back to their houses and apartments and mobile homes on ordinary streets in ordinary towns. They make oatmeal for their families for breakfast and spaghetti for dinner and chat with one another in front yards about what have become ordinary moral questions.

"That elderly lady with the bad leg wandered away from the nursing home on the next block again last night. It was hours before anyone even noticed she was missing. The staff just doesn't pay attention to their patients. Do you think I should call the authorities or mind my own business?"

The moral choices that we must make are the natural consequences of living here and now. We'd like nothing more than to get up and go to work and go home and be with family and socialize on earth as it is in heaven. No confrontations. No backs against the wall. No sneaking suspicion that we're being asked to decide whether to wimp out or stand up. Or when or whether it's right to compromise our convictions for the sake of harmony.

"My sister is divorcing her husband because he wants to control her life. He won't listen to reason or go for counseling. Should I condone what she's doing?"

WOMEN TODAY

Women in our society do face tougher moral choices than ever. One reason is that society's view of what's right has changed. Secularists have won their freedom to be humanistic and relativistic and compromise themselves to death. Because their words resound with authority, we wonder. *Are the black-and-white values I was fed during my growing up years still valid?* For they seem narrow now, the product of unenlightened minds. So we ask ourselves: *Do I have antiquated morals? Or* has the line between good and evil been blurred by the sweat from mankind's greedy, decadent palms?

Once, sex before marriage was anathema. Now, more do than don't. If Grandma found herself unmarried and pregnant, her options would probably have been to give birth to the baby, give him or her up for adoption, or have an illegal abortion.

Things were very different for a friend of mine. A fairly new Christian, she could have an easy-to-obtain legal abortion, place the baby for adoption, or raise the child herself as a single parent with little stigma.

The enormous moral and ethical ramifications of the twentieth century explosion of knowledge in scientific and technological fields is a second reason we women face tougher moral choices. Should we have amniocentesis? What if we learn that the baby in our womb is malformed? Do we abort? Suppose we learn through genetic counseling that we could pass a disease in our lineage to our children. Do we marry but not bear children? Stay single? Marry and bear children, leaving their health up to God?

What if we are unable to bear a child except through artificial insemination? Is it permissible as long as the donor is our mate? But our mate may be infertile. Would it be adultery to be implanted with donor sperm? Is artificial insemination playing God?

When Marconi obtained his patent for the wireless, he couldn't have imagined the dilemma a twentieth-century disc jockey in the Pacific Northwest would face as a result. "A fair amount of the songs I was supposed to play had 'let's go to bed' lyrics. I struggled with guilt every time I put one on. Finally I decided I'd have to quit."

Amniocentesis and artificial insemination and genetic counseling and genetic engineering and AIDS didn't exist in Bible times so there are no "thou shalt nots" to guide us. God didn't include in Scripture a set of commandments stamped: "Not to be opened until the twentieth century A.D." So when we sweat to know what to do, we wonder whether science and technology have outrun God and we've been abandoned to decide for ourselves.

Third, the women's movement has confused us. The cry for female liberation seems to imply, for one thing, that women have the exclusive right to decide the use of their bodies as well as the lifestyle that suits them. "Any limit on her decision-making process is thought to be treating her as incapable or immature."[1]

The media resounds their cry from TV talk show platforms, magazine headlines, and bestselling book titles. Liberationists have redefined women's roles and redefined as well what success is. What are we to think?

A fourth reason is that we can no longer count on the church to be prelates of our moral behavior. For it shows signs of an old malady—moral adaptation. "Organized Christianity still has not learned . . . the church still too often is a tail wagged by the dog of the world."[2]

QUESTIONS AND ANSWERS

Theologians disagree so loudly and violently that they create a cacophony in our ears. Ask the church a question and get a plethora of answers. *Should a Christian divorce? On what grounds? May divorced people remarry? Are there restrictions?*

Our own local church may be as unbending as the stereotype of an Amish elder—or may dismiss our moral questions with a wave of the hand the way a pastor I know did. "There are no gray areas. Moral choices for Christians are black and white. What to do is all there in Scripture."

It's no wonder the women sitting across from me in retreat

centers are confused. It's no wonder I have been confused. What we need, first of all, is for someone to take our hand and smile into our eyes. "The fact that you don't know how to resolve this doesn't mean you are a bad Christian. It's a natural result of living in the world as it is right now."

Another reason our choices are so complex is because who we are and what we do has been completely redefined, and as a result, so have the choices we must make. Instead of spending their days with bake ovens and sewing machines, more than half of our sex spends their days over computers or cash registers. Because we're in the workplace either full or part time, we have to decide whether or not to have dinner with our male boss when we're working late, and what is and is not truth in advertising.

We serve on school boards and planning committees with non-Christians and must decide how to cope with secular humanistic concepts when we review textbooks and how to speak Christianly at a town council meeting. We get up petitions and are asked to participate in public protests and must decide if we will or not.

While our earlier counterparts likely served the church by either singing in the choir, playing the organ, teaching Sunday School, sewing for missions, visiting in homes, or arranging covered-dish suppers, we have assumed new positions of leadership. We are pastors of Christian education and even of local congregations themselves. We are church staff counselors. We are pastors of women's ministries or assist those who are. Women look to us for help in knowing what to decide. We must have answers.

We who are married have more family responsibility than our predecessors, and that responsibility brings with it moral choices. A wife may manage the family finances because she's better at it than her husband, and must decide about indebtedness. She may do the taxes, and must decide what to declare; hire people to remodel the house, and decide what expectations of them are fair.

More of us discipline our children instead of waiting until Daddy gets home. So we have to decide now whether or not our son should listen to the rock tape he borrowed from a friend or whether he should return it immediately.

We'll probably decide with our husbands whether or not to send our child to a public or Christian school, but whether or not to homeschool him or her is likely to be more our choice than his. We are the ones who must switch from mother to teacher every weekday morning, so we must know plainly what we think.

MARRIED WOMEN AND DECISIONS

More than 15 percent of us head up families alone. We are women who are divorced or widowed with young children, wives of incapacitated husbands, single women who have borne children or adopted them, unmarried women who care for younger relatives. We must make every ethical choice for ourselves, from "Which films do I let my teenage son see?" to "What in the world do I tell him about masturbation?"

Many of us are single longer or are alone after a divorce. We too must make all our own moral choices. We may be lonely and hear about all those others who are having "relationships." The idea has become as acceptable as wearing jeans. *Is it really out of the question for me?*

It doesn't get easier as we get older, either. Many retired women I know do not live enfolded protectively in an extended family, tribal fashion. Some do have grown children who care, but often they're across town or across the state and are busy landscaping their yards and chauffeuring the children to ball games.

One widow I know struggled for weeks to decide whether or not it was right to fire someone in her employ, even though it seemed necessary for several reasons. My friend kept worrying that she would be uncharitable because her employee had no money and could become destitute quickly.

How *do* we make moral choices when right and wrong isn't plainly stated in the Bible? Do the best we can after prayer? Go by gut feeling? Follow the advice of a Christian we respect?

Is it possible that God has not left us to push our way through the thicket on our own?

He has not. The eternal God our Creator has made us a promise and has repeated it so we will make no mistake.

"I will *instruct* you and *teach* you in the way you should go; I will *counsel* you and watch over you" (Ps. 32:8, italics added).

"For this God is our God forever and ever; He will be our *guide* even to the end" (48:14, *italics added*).

"But when He, the Spirit of Truth, comes, He will *guide* you into all truth" (John 16:13, *italics added*).

God instructs.

God teaches.

God counsels.

God guides

... forever and ever ... even to the end.

That is the promise.

This book explains *how* He instructs, guides, teaches, and counsels in times like these.

"Ask where the good way is, and walk in it, and you will find rest for your souls" (Jer. 6:16).

1. Gretchen Gabeline Hull, "Abortion and the Christian Community: The Challenge to Be Change Agents," *reNews*, March 1992, p. 8-3.
2. Randy C. Alcorn, *Christians in the Wake of the Sexual Revolution* (Portland, Ore.: Multnomah Press, 1985), p. 53.

Thinking for Ourselves

TWO ❦

On our way to womanhood we were taught how to choose clothing that flattered us, food that nourished us, curriculum that educated us, and a lifestyle that was best for us. But we were not taught how to make moral choices when no absolutes existed.

That's not a reflection on those who brought us up. Even the most well-taught women I know have had more questions than answers. Like the mother who'd just discovered that her son was homosexual, we think: *nothing prepared me for this.*

GRAY AREAS

I was about forty the first time I faced the fact that I was not prepared to make moral choices in so-called "gray" areas. My teenage son and I were standing in the kitchen. "Tell me again. Why do we believe that Christians shouldn't dance?" he asked.

Could he tell how uncertain I felt as I repeated what I'd been taught? "Because of suggestive lyrics, provocative music, and the fact that it can lead to other things."

He listened silently and then frowned slightly. "I just wondered," was all he said before he walked away.

That moment I was unmasked — at least to myself — as a woman who didn't have convictions of her own on nonabsolutes. There had been no certainty behind my words because I hadn't thought through "to dance or not to dance" as well as a plethora of other issues that confronted me. I felt half-formed.

I know now that many women feel that way. Often they've whispered their confusion to me. To find answers, we've journeyed back through their lives. What we've discovered is that in addition to *external* reasons for our confusion over moral issues (the times in which we live), every woman has her own *internal* reasons.

The months after my own crisis, I kept flicking through the first three decades of my life to understand. In the first scene, I saw myself as an only child in a single-parent family who depended on "Mama says."

She was my authority and security so I nodded wholehearted affirmation to her moral code. For example: "It's wrong to drink alcoholic beverages," she taught me. Of course, that settled it: drinking was wrong.

From her I learned that marital unfaithfulness was wrong too. Even though my father had been in a mental institution since I was two years old, Mama refused to have affairs with the men who asked her.

We knew that her women friends, widowed or deserted, were having affairs. "Their mamas are doing wrong," my mother told me. "It's wrong to sleep with a man who's not your husband."

Besides Mama, during the first decade of my life, I learned about right and wrong from the church. That code centered on the Ten Commandments that I memorized in Sunday School.

To me, they were thundering pronouncements. The idea of breaking one of them made me shiver. I also heard the softer, gentler commandments about loving other people, but how to apply these seemed vague and blurry.

With my teen years came the desire to be accepted by my peers, but their moral code was definitely in conflict with Mama's. A date and his family wanted me to go to a bar. *If I refuse? If Mama finds out?*

Feeling as guilty as though I were stealing from the cash register, I went, drank a Coke, and agonized every clock-tick of the fifteen minutes or so that we were there.

I'd now added a third authority to "Mama says" and "The church says"—one that now carried the most weight.

Mama died when I was twenty-one. A few months later, I met and married John. The man I loved became a fourth authority and in the third decade of my life, it was his voice that superseded all others.

A FINAL AUTHORITY

One Sunday evening at age thirty, I kneeled at my bedside to ask Christ into my life. When I arose, I was a daughter of God. John was converted to faith in Jesus Christ not long afterward. Now we both had a final authority—God Almighty. But I still wanted to look to John to decide what the godly thing was to do.

A few years later, John and I entered full-time ministry

with a stateside missionary organization. In that capacity, John pastored rural churches and I worked beside him. Now I subscribed to a new moral authority—the mission board. At that time, their tenets, for example, included no Sunday comics. It was understood that we were to refrain from any behavior that might be a "stumbling block" to someone in the community.

For the next decade that we served as missionaries, I didn't have to think through moral issues for myself. I was committed to take a conservative stand. What was there to think about?

Then because of John's ill health we resigned from that work, packed up bikes and beds, and left the parsonage behind us. No mission board as authority. Now I had to decide for myself what to read on Sunday and what entertainment was morally acceptable for our family on Saturday night, as well as a plethora of issues that were emerging on the scene.

Even though John was my husband and had strong moral views, he wanted me to think for myself. Even if a choice had to be made mutually because it affected both of us and he'd make the final decision, I had to know what I thought.

The idea terrified me. *What if I decide wrongly?* A friend's reaction in her own situation summed up how at least part of me felt. "I hate the idea of having to make moral choices in so-called gray areas. I think maybe there are absolutes for everything and I'm missing what they are."

Hear the words of a woman in *The Joy Luck Club*. "In the end I would be so confused, because I never believed there was ever any one right answer, yet there were many wrong ones. So whenever I said, 'You decide,' or 'I don't care,' or 'Either way is fine with me,' Ted would say in his impatient voice, 'No, *you* decide. You can't have it both ways, none of the responsibility, none of the blame.' "[1]

The prospect of deciding for myself also excited me. Part of me *wanted* to know what *she* thought.

My mental journey back through the decades had helped me see the reason for my dichotomy: I'd always counted on others to do my thinking for me and that felt safe. But I also felt immature.

UNDERSTAND YOUR RELUCTANCE

Every woman who is having trouble knowing what she thinks needs to make the same kind of interior journey in order to understand her own reluctance.

We may have been raised to be dependent. "My father was very authoritarian," one woman told me. "His word was law. We didn't discuss issues. He spoke and I obeyed. So I grew up unable to take the initiative to think issues through for myself."

A parent may have believed that to be feminine, a woman must be dependent. Or we may feel incapable because a parent's fear for our well-being kept us children for longer than was healthy.

We are pleasers. A businesswoman friend told me, "I wanted desperately to get my dad's approval, but all that was important to him was financial success. So I set out to accomplish that, never mind the cost to my family. I see now it was wrong to sacrifice them." So long as she was bent on pleasing Dad, she couldn't cultivate her own set of standards.

Need for self-worth may have demanded acquiescence. That was true of me. Approval and acceptance were more important than anything. It was also true of Connie.* Now 37, she recalled her own younger years. "I agreed with everybody. I

---

*In some cases, names and identities have been changed.

acted as though I was all for a thing—even when my conscience bothered me badly."

Adults who disagreed may have confused us. If Mom went to church and endorsed the Bible as the Word of God but Dad discounted it completely, what were we to think—especially if Dad taunted Mom and others like her? *Play it safe; don't take sides. Just slide through.*

For a friend, the challenge to know what she thought came during her years at a liberal arts college. "All of a sudden, everyone's hitting you with all these issues. I believe God allowed me to go through those years of turmoil because it made me think. It's out of those circumstances that convictions grow."

Our church may have decided for us. Katie was raised in a church that had a long list of do's and don'ts. "If I questioned a particular rule, my mother told me to just *do* it, and I was chastised for asking questions."

We may think that submission to our husbands requires it. This subject will be discussed in detail in chapter 10.

Our personalities lean toward passivity. Some women I've met are naturally assertive and plunge ahead. On the other hand many (and that included me) agonize over things like whether to play bingo at the request of our new mother-in-law. *My own mother would be appalled. How do I feel? I'm not sure.*

Past moral choices were disastrous so we no longer trust ourselves. Maxie shook her head. "I feel so guilty about past bad decisions I've made that when something confronts me I want to go to bed and pull the covers over my head. Why shouldn't I feel that way? After all, I let myself be talked into having two abortions by the time I was twenty-five."

Some said that until crisis came, they were passive.

"I began to think about what I believed after my husband walked out for another woman."

"It was when my children hit their teen years that I began to think hard about moral issues because I had to."

OPINIONS OR FEELINGS

There are those of us who have no trouble knowing what we think. We could recite a litany of opinions: "Abortion is wrong and infertility treatments are right and. . . . "

In some cases, however, we are simply going by "gut feelings." It's important to ask ourselves: have I thought these issues through carefully and come to an informed decision?

Of course, not every choice we make has an ethical connotation. Deciding whether to wear your green jacket or your gray one or whether to stop at the cleaners on the way home or wait until Saturday are decisions that, in themselves, have no ethical implications. We make these on the basis of personal preference and expedience. But whether or not to indulge in sexual fantasies must be decided on the basis of our ethics.

Ethics is the process we use when we establish a set of principles to determine what's right and wrong. We do it by analyzing, evaluating, reflecting, and finally, deciding what we think. Christian ethics are based, not on secular philosophy, but on the Bible.

Morals are the everyday decisions we make and the actions we take based on what we see as right and wrong. If we conclude that stealing includes time as well as money or goods, that's an ethical guideline by which to live. So if we choose to work instead of taking a two-hour lunch when the boss is gone, we've made a moral choice based on that ethical guideline.

Our ethics are based on our *convictions*. More than beliefs, which are ideas we hold intellectually, convictions are that which we hold deeply and wholeheartedly and of which we are convinced. Convictions differ from *preferences* which are simply what we'd rather do, and from *opinions* which are what we think but are not based on what we accept as irrefutable.

So we are called to make moral choices based on ethical guidelines. These guidelines, in turn, are based on principles from the Word of God that we've fleshed out and applied by a Spirit-enlightened mind.

That's important because every conviction isn't necessarily good. Skinheads who harangue against blacks say they do so because they are convinced that minority group is inferior to whites. Adolf Hitler was convinced that Jews were pollutants and exterminated 6 million of them.

Some may still secretly wonder if the whole idea of a woman forming personal convictions about what her moral choices should be is some latter-day departure from the truth. Has it been born out of the echoes of Friedan and Steinem and translated into Christian? Or is it biblical for women to know what they think in the moral sphere and live by their convictions?

EXAMPLES FROM SCRIPTURE

First, we have examples of women in the Bible who did just that. Queen Esther is one who has been lauded through the centuries for the choice she made. Raised by her uncle Mordecai because she was an orphan, Esther was chosen by King Xerxes to become his queen, replacing Vashti who had fallen out of favor. Mordecai forbid Esther to let the king's court know she was a Jewess.

Mordecai refused to pay homage to a man named Haman who'd been honored by the king. To retaliate, Haman fabricated to Xerxes that Jews were a threat to his kingdom. The king gave Haman permission to lead a movement to wipe out that people and seize their property.

That's when Esther had to make a moral choice. Would she listen to her substitute father Mordecai and intercede before the king for the Jews? But she knew that appearing before Xerxes without first being summoned was against the law and the punishment was death. The personal stakes were too high to simply acquiesce to Mordecai's wishes. She'd have to know for herself what her moral responsibility was.

Decide she did. "I will go to the king, even though it is against the law. And if I perish, I perish" (Es. 4:16). As a result of her action, the Jews were saved from annihilation.

Another woman in Scripture who made a tough moral choice is Ruth. Her story is not one of kings and courts and edicts, but of peasants and unselfish love.

Ruth and Orpah were the daughters-in-law of Naomi, a Jewess who, with her husband Elimelech, had emigrated from Israel to Moab during a famine. After Elimelech's death, Naomi, Ruth, and Orpah (who were now also widows) set out to return to Israel.

On the way, Naomi stopped. "Go back, each of you, to your mother's home. May the Lord show kindness to you, as you have shown to your dead and to me. May the Lord grant that each of you will find rest in the home of another husband" (Ruth 1:8-9).

After tearfully objecting, Orpah obeyed her mother-in-law's wishes. Ruth, however, continued to cling to Naomi, who pressed her further to go home.

Should she obey Naomi? If she refused and accompanied her mother-in-law, wasn't it unlikely that she'd find another husband in a strange country where she knew no one? On the other hand, didn't Naomi need her?

Ruth was convinced. " 'Where you go I will go, and where you stay I will stay. Your people will be my people and your

God my God. . . . '

"When Naomi realized that Ruth was determined to go with her, she stopped urging her" (vv. 16-18). Because of her choice, Ruth was the one who, until her marriage to Boaz, supported Naomi by the sweaty work of gleaning in the fields.

Second, besides the examples of women, there is the teaching of the Bible itself.

Women are persons. That's the way they're described in Scripture — as persons who are female.

Women are created in the image of God. Keep in mind that where "man" is used generically, it refers to "mankind" — the human race in general.

"So God created man in His own image, in the image of God He created him; male and female He created them" (Gen. 1:27). We're correct to conclude, therefore, that "the female is as much a bearer of the image of God as is the male."[2]

Christ removed human differences. The New Testament goes on to make plain the fact that the Gospel, with all its implications, applies to all humans indiscriminately. "There is neither Jew nor Greek, slave nor free, male nor female, for you are all one in Christ Jesus" (Gal. 3:28).

Women were given responsibility. "It is man as male and female who receives the royal commission from God to rule the earth:* 'Rule over the fish of the sea and the birds of the air and over every living creature that moves on the ground' (Gen. 1:28). . . . In their original setting . . . these words from the mouth of the Creator God were given to the female and to the male, to both of them together."[3]

Women are accountable. As females created in the image of God with a free will and, therefore, with the ability to act independently and commanded to rule over the earth, we are morally responsible for our actions. "So then, each of us will give an account of himself [or herself] to God" (Rom. 14:12).

Therefore: *this graying, 5'4" second-generation Rumanian Swede is a responsible female human being created in the image of God and is personally accountable to Him.*

The concept was still a near stranger to me when I was called to make what was for me a particularly unsettling moral choice. I had *thought* I knew what was right, but was intimidated when my stand was challenged by a church's women's group.

For several years, I had been visiting in a nursing home where many residents were retarded or had other mental problems. Each month I baked cakes for the birthdays of the fifty or so who lived there.

Then my husband and I were going to leave the state to begin a new church. I accepted the offer of a women's group to assume responsibility for my nursing home ministry.

When I returned, their representative told me that the women didn't want to continue the ministry—"because you can't evangelize them." Their intimation was clear: this was not the Lord's work.

First I felt angry. Then I felt intimidated. Had I deceived myself? Was I wasting time and money? Was I too timid to take on a "real" ministry? If it was God's work, I had to be convinced for myself so I could continue in the face of criticism. But how could I decide what was right?

1. Amy Tan, *The Joy Luck Club* (New York: Ivy Books, 1989), p. 126.
2. Ronald and Beverly Allen, *Liberated Traditionalism* (Portland, Ore.: Multnomah Press, 1985), p. 97.
3. Ibid., p. 100.

Does the Bible Have the Answers?

THREE ❧

*D*espite years of study, I found myself hard put to find directives for specific situations in the Bible. Finally I came to see that God has not given us a thumb-indexed, moral encyclopedia. Instead, He has gifted us with a collection of divinely inspired works that provide us with His perspective on life.

"Norms"—a word that originally meant "a carpenter's square or rule." The Bible enables us to square our lives morally with God's. The first way it does that is through the Ten Commandments and New Testament directives.[1]

LAW AND GRACE

The Ten Commandments found in Exodus 20:1-17 are the only moral laws spoken directly by God Himself and written by His own finger on stone tablets. Not merely a set of rules, as I thought in Sunday School, they stated plainly how the Israelites were to live if they wanted God to keep His promise of protection and abundance. The first four governed their behavior toward God; the last six, their behavior in society.

Are women supposed to live by these commandments today? Gentile women?

The Bible itself plainly answers that question.

"You are not under law, but under grace" (Rom. 6:14).

Not that we're to chuck the Ten Commandments as obsolete. Thundered on the mountain and meant to echo throughout history, they are definitely religious and social standards. Of the ten, all but "Remember the Sabbath Day by keeping it holy," are stated in the New Testament (Ex. 20:8). But they are not rules we must doggedly keep to win God's smile. Christ kept them for us.

Jesus did endorse the commandments and interpreted them as standards to apply—not just to what we *do*—but to what we *think* as well. He perceived them as hitting at the heart of who we are. Consider this one for example: "Anyone who looks at a woman lustfully has already committed adultery with her in his heart" (Matt. 5:28).

Was He talking about an admiring glance at a bronzed, shapely woman in tight jeans? "The man Jesus described looked at the woman *for the purpose of feeding his inner sensual appetites* as a substitute for the act."[2] A woman who continually fantasizes about going to a motel with a man in the office—imagining them in bed together—is the female counterpart of the male Jesus cited.

The commandments definitely are standards for women today. But since they're general in nature, every woman in every era must decide how they apply to a specific situation.

You shall have no other gods before Me . . . you shall not make for yourself an idol. To a woman in Bible times this meant that devotion to Baal and Asheroth were anathema. To a woman today, it might mean "By thinking *career* breakfast, lunch, and dinner, I'm turning it into a god."

You shall not kill literally means *You shall not murder* — premeditatively take another person's life, because the real meaning of the Hebrew word "kill" is "murder."

ABORTION

Lynda is a nurse friend who spent several years working in labor and delivery and doing the complete opposite of that commandment by helping bring life into the world. "I never saw a birth that didn't awe me."

She was transferred to the exam room — and then abortion became legal. Required to assist in as many as thirty or forty abortions a month, she "tried to think in every direction about it. Since it has to be done, maybe I could do a little counseling afterward." There was no opportunity to counsel beforehand, since the women had been treated by their physicians the evening before so they'd be dilated when they went for an abortion the next day. There was no turning back.

Occasionally Lynda was able to counsel one of the younger girls. But the process became more and more offensive to her. "Abortion was definitely taking a life. It was killing premeditatively." She put in for a transfer but none was available. One of the doctors, sensitive to her repugnancy of the process, began cleaning the equipment after abortions and also putting the sacks of remains in specimen bottles.

"One day I looked in the basin where the surgical tools had been put and floating in it was a tiny foot. I couldn't take it. I started crying and called the supervisor. I said that I had to get out. This time a position in another department was open, and I took it."

In addition to the Old Testament commandments, God also provides guidance through plain directives in the New Testament. Here are a couple of examples for us to read and study.

"Do not store up for yourselves treasures on earth. . . . But store up for yourselves treasures in heaven" (Matt. 6:19-20). *Buy an antique table to add to my collection or eyeglasses for a pensioner friend who just broke hers and can't get new ones?* Jesus makes the answer plain.

"Give to Caesar what is Caesar's and to God what is God's" (Mark 12:17). *That means obedience of the civil law — on the freeway, for example.*

New Testament letters also contain commands given by inspiration of the Holy Spirit.

"Honor God with your body" (1 Cor. 6:20). Jennie said that she ate to fill an inner void and had gained thirty pounds. *This is definitely not honoring God with my body, and I need to get help.*

"See that no one is sexually immoral" (Heb. 12:16). *That means me. I can't use my need for love as an excuse.*

"Don't show favoritism" (James 2:1). *I'll welcome the new family across the street the way I would any other even though part of me wants to buy into the stereotypes about that particular minority.*

A good many of the choices we make, however, will be based on principles. This is the second way the Bible enables us to square our lives with God's.

A principle is a fundamental truth on which others are based, such as "All men are created equal." Some principles in the Bible are stated plainly, like, "Do to others as you would have them do to you" (Luke 6:31). This is called the Golden Rule.

We'll find out how to use these to make moral choices in chapter 5.

PRINCIPLES

Why principles? The Bible is a book for all centuries and all cultures, and a collection of laws simply won't do. The Masai people of Kenya, Africa for example, consider it wrong for husband and wife to hold hands in public. American women at the turn of the twentieth century considered it immoral to show their ankles. Today we need to know whether or not it's acceptable to wear a bikini on the beach or shorts in the shopping mall. So God gave guidelines for Masai women, Victorian women, and modern Western women to apply in their cultural situations.

The idea of formulating principles frightened this girl from Brooklyn. I still wanted to open the Bible and find the answer stated plainly. "Yes, Marion, it's acceptable to have dinner alone with an old male friend on your trip back East."

But God wanted me to decide based on His guidelines. And He'd provided a variety of kinds of biblical literature for me to use.

The examples of Jesus. It's important to keep in mind that situations in Bible times were different from situations now. Our country is not occupied by Roman soldiers; we do not have to deal with religious authorities like the Pharisees and Sadducees. But still, situations that Jesus experienced may typify situations we go through now. The character qualities and ethical choices He made in His situations are often transferable to our own.

Examples of biblical characters. Esther and Ruth exemplify women who chose others' good over personal safety. What about Abraham's determination to find a wife who wasn't an ungodly Canaanite for his son Isaac? His action to bring that about by sending his servant to find a suitable bride? (Gen. 24) He clearly is an example for parents—not to send a servant to Nahor—but to provide Christian friends of the opposite sex—perhaps in a church youth group.

Whether we wear robes or jeans, Joseph's example of refus-ing to go to bed with the wife of his master Potiphar sends a clear message through the centuries. "He left his cloak in her hand and ran out of the house" (39:12).

Negative examples are just as important as positive ones. Moses' anger at the Egyptian who was beating a Hebrew was justified. Killing the Egyptian was not. We can take Moses' deadly explosion as a warning to express our anger in a moral fashion.

Parables. You're not likely to be traveling on the road from Jerusalem to Jericho the way the Good Samaritan was and find a Jew (his natural enemy) lying on the side of the road half dead (Luke 10:25-37).

You *are* likely to have a neighbor who's been less than friendly. As a matter of fact, you've hardly been able to have a pleasant conversation with her.

She becomes ill and there's no one to help. The clear, supra-historical teaching of Jesus in this story-illustration is to act mercifully—bake a casserole and do the laundry perhaps.

Poetry, like the Psalms, is inspired song-lyrics, but state-ments about God and man often can be used to support guidelines. Take Psalm 100 (KJV).

Make a joyful noise unto the Lord, all ye lands.
  Serve the Lord with gladness;
come before His presence with singing.

  Know ye that the Lord He is God: it is He that hath made us; and not we ourselves; we are His people and the sheep of His pasture.

  Enter into His gates with thanksgiving and into His courts with praise: be thankful unto Him, and bless His name.

  For the Lord is good; His mercy is everlasting; and

His truth endureth to all generations.

One conclusion you might reach based on this poem is *God deserves to be worshiped. If government refused to allow me to do so, I would have to challenge the restriction.*

Proverbs. These are short, pithy general observations about human life found in the Book of Proverbs but also scattered throughout the Bible. They also can be used to support teaching literature. Solomon emphasized the importance of living morally and pointed out different ways to do that.

"Go to the ant, you sluggard; consider its ways and be wise" (6:6). *Is my husband right when he criticizes me for not getting my housework done?* Not if it's because I have a handicapped child and a sick mother-in-law to take care of. But if my daily schedule begins with a neighborhood coffee klatsch followed by favorite TV shows followed by mall browsing, he probably is. That's definitely not ant-like behavior.

How do we get started so we'll become facile in using Scripture as a basis for our convictions? One way is to investigate what the Bible has to say about a particular issue when we face it. We'll do that later.

PERSONAL ETHICS

The other is to begin to construct a personal ethic, one commandment and one principle at a time. Your personal ethic will help you form convictions. You'll formulate this ethic slowly and gradually, often as part of your regular Bible study.

How in the world do I begin? For me the answer was my journal. I'd begun journaling when I became interested in writing for publication. In time, that notebook became a place where I thought through problems. Daily, I also recorded insights into Scripture. So it was natural to use it to collect passages that address right and wrong.

For example, during daily devotions, when I came across a passage that contained a moral guideline, I wrote it down. Take Matthew 6:33: "Seek first [God's] kingdom and His righteousness, and all these things will be given you as well."

My entry would be something like this: "Marion, do what you believe is the godly action in your work even if it threatens your security. God will provide your needs." Gradually I found my journal growing rich with such statements. Every month or so, I review what I've written in my journal, bringing together the new moral guidelines I've discovered.

I meet many women who journal—at least from time to time. So that's a natural way for them to begin. Other women prefer to use a notebook set aside only for the purpose of fulfilling a personal ethic.

You'll probably begin haltingly and with uncertainty. But the delight you experience as you gain insight will make you want to know more. In addition, your Bible will begin to become *your* moral guide and not simply a treasured Book.

As your value system grows, so will your personhood, and with it new self-respect. No longer will you want merely to be acted upon: *If he comes home and apologizes for abusing me, it'll be a sign I should stay with him. If he doesn't, I'll take it as a sign I should leave him.*

Elisabeth Elliot's words will make absolute sense: "Why did He not summarize all the rules in one book, and all the basic doctrines in another? . . . Think of the squabbling and perplexity we would have been spared. And think of the crop of dwarfs He would have reared!"[1]

He did not spare us. He wants us to reach maturity. He has so arranged things that . . . we shall be forced to think.

1. Milton L. Rudnick, *Christian Ethics for Today* (Grand Rapids: Baker

Book House, 1979), p. 45.

2. Warren Wiersbe, *The Bible Exposition Commentary*, Vol. 1 (Wheaton, Ill.: Victor Books, 1989), p. 24.

3. Elisabeth Elliot, *The Liberty of Obedience* (Waco, Texas: Word Books, 1968), p. 57.

Our Decision-Making Center

FOUR 🥀

*E*very woman does have a decision-making center. Not a supertronic computer command post where she can punch in a question and receive God's answer:

"We can't afford any more children. Is it acceptable for me to have my tubes tied?"

Our decision-making center is an intricate, interior, God-given combination of human faculties provided specifically for that purpose. They are:

1. Mind
2. Conscience
3. Emotions
4. Will
5. Spirit

Mind. Unlike Pooh Bear, whose "head was stuffed with fluff,"[1] our brain is a three-pound wonder. It includes conscious and subconscious mind; intellect—which includes the ability to reason, compare, perform logic, perceive, and understand; memory; and imagination, or the ability to produce mental images and generate ideas. Clearly our minds are masterpieces and gifts from God.

"I'm just learning that I do have the ability to think things through," Shirley told me at a retreat. "That's because nearly every day my dad told me I didn't have any brains." I meet women like her often. Over tea, I urge them to see the error of what they've been taught and accept the truth about themselves. Often they need someone to help them through the process.

There's another reason we may recoil at the thought of creative thinking or logic as part of our decision-making process. *Trust our minds when they're so corrupt?* We may even cite biblical proof: "The sinful mind is hostile to God. It does not submit to God's law, nor can it do so" (Rom. 8:7).

True. Since the Fall, our thinking has been influenced by the serpent. But that doesn't mean our brain is a deteriorated organ, a throw-away invaded at Eden by some spiritual AIDS-like virus, making it incapable of godly use.

For at the new birth we acquired the ability to develop a new way of thinking. "You were taught . . . to put off your old self, which is being corrupted by its deceitful desires; to be made new in the attitude of your minds; and to put on the new self, created to be like God in true righteousness and holiness" (Eph. 4:22-24). Now we have the ability to align our thoughts with the Spirit of God.

Instead of telling us to put our brain in storage because we may think wrongly, Scripture *urges* us to think. " 'Come now, let us reason together,' says the Lord" (Isa. 1:18). The word "reason" is a legal term used of arguing, convincing, or deciding a case in court. "Christians cannot afford the *privilege of ideas* without the *expense of thinking.*"[2]

CHAPTER AND VERSE

Lauren Littauer Briggs had no chapter or verse she could turn to when deciding how aggressively the attending physician should treat her eighty-five-year-old grandmother who had been found unresponsive in bed and who was dying of cancer. If her grandmother stopped breathing, should she be put on a respirator? If she experienced cardiac arrest, should she be stimulated?

The only relative present, Lauren had to make a decision. Was she or was she not bound to tell the physician to use aggressive medical techniques? Did it make a difference that her grandmother was eighty-five and not nineteen? What was the prognosis of the cancer from which her grandmother was suffering? What decision would her grandmother want her to make? How did she sense God was leading her?

"Randy, [Lauren's husband] and I knew we were speaking for Grammy and her children when we said, 'No respirator, no heart machine, and no extraordinary measures to keep her alive.' "'

What precautions can we take so that, if we must stand in a hospital corridor and decide about our loved one, our thought processes will be the most pre-Fall they can be?

• Remain sensitive to our tendency toward self-centeredness. *Part of me wants to arrive at the easiest, most expedient conclusion.*

• See that the renewing of our minds remains a lifetime priority. *My decisions will be godly only if my philosophy is centered on Your character.*

• Keep reminding ourselves that what we think is only part of the decision-making process. *I want to use all the decision-making gifts You've provided, Lord.*

• See ourselves as learners. *You expect me to make my very best effort, not to demonstrate perfect logic.*

We may be unconvinced that God could be satisfied with less than a perfect moral choice on our part. As a new believer, I was—especially when I read, "Be ye therefore perfect, even as your Father which is in heaven is perfect" (Matt. 5:48, KJV).

I was relieved when I read the Amplified Version. "You, therefore, must be perfect ... [that is, grow into complete maturity of godliness in mind and character]." I was to *grow* in maturity. I was a learner and would be one all my life. God knew that. I was to make the best decision of which I was capable now.

In what specific ways is a woman meant to use her mind to form a conviction? By collecting information and evaluating it; brainstorming alternatives; delving into memory to provide past experiences that might give insight; using logic to separate truth from error; and using reason to formulate premises and come to conclusions.

Conscience. What is this much misunderstood human faculty? "Your conscience is you, those elements of your psyche ... which deal with issues of right and wrong.... Your conscience is a monitor built into you which is itself part of you."[4]

When it comes to forming convictions, a woman's conscience is meant to be her natural guide of what's right and what's wrong. The trouble is, conscience simply isn't trustworthy in its natural state. For our inner monitor knows only what it's been taught—and what it's been taught may not have been wholly biblical.

Several women I know were taught that wrong was right when they were growing up.

"My mother taught me how to shoplift," one told me. "The only sin was to get caught."

"My parents drank and gave me beer when I was a toddler. As a child, I could have had as much as I wanted. As far as I could tell, this was just a way to have a good time."

Other women's consciences are overscrupulous because of their upbringing. "Talking about sex at all was absolutely taboo in our home. So when I married, I felt guilty talking about it with my husband." Or as one who was raised on the familiar "don'ts" said, "The first time I went to see a movie I expected the theater to crumble on top of me."

UNTRUSTWORTHY CONSCIENCE

Since conscience isn't trustworthy, should we consult it at all? Paul utilized *his* conscience when determining his moral behavior. "Our conscience testifies that we have conducted ourselves in the world, and especially in our relations with you, in the holiness and sincerity that are from God" (2 Cor. 1:12).

If we ignore our conscience and do what we sense is wrong, it hauls us into court and condemns us, professor Garry Friesen points out. As a result, we feel guilty.[5] So we're to maintain a clear conscience (Rom. 13:5; 1 Peter 3:16).

But what if our conscience is overscrupulous or tyrannical? Are we to spend our lives doing what it asks if it's been taught unbiblically?

Hardly. *God does not mean us to allow wrongly taught consciences to remain our moral authority.* He does want us to reclaim our consciences. We're to ask God to give us insight where it has been wrongly taught. He'll do that gradually, helping us compare error with biblical principles.

While conscience is in the process of being retaught, we may be confused. It heaps guilt on us if we try to talk about sexual matters, yet we're coming to suspect it's wrong when it insists: *It's wrong to talk about sex so don't participate in a women's class that discusses the subject.*

At times like this, it's helpful to talk over the state of our conscience with a mature Christian. As truth takes root within, we'll know: *God created human sexuality and called it good. So it's OK to discuss sexual functions in the right context.*

In addition, so conscience will be most effective, keep it clear and clean. That means we'll have to take action—rejecting false guilt and alleviating real guilt by confessing sin. It's the blood of Christ, says the writer of Hebrews, that cleanses our consciences from acts that lead to death, so we may serve the living God (9:14).

How do we use conscience in forming a conviction? As a starting place: *What is my innate moral sense in this area?* Always reserve judgment, measuring what conscience says against revealed truth.

Emotion. A catalyst, emotion comes from a word that means "to stir up, agitate," and is defined as a subjective reaction to a situation. Lynda's subjective reaction to performing abortions was one of revulsion. My response to the women who believed visiting in the nursing home was a waste of time was one of anger.

The trouble is, we women are accused of "being overemotional"—of letting our emotions dictate our response. That generalization, like most, is inaccurate. Women are not alike simply because they are all female. Some of us do respond reflexively with our emotions, like a woman at a retreat I led recently who said that life continually moved her—either to laughter or to tears.

But suppose we are that kind of person? Should my friend Karla distrust her overwhelming feelings of sorrow when she sees ragged, dirty children? Of course not. She should realize, though, that what she feels is only *part* of the decision-making faculties God has given her. Therefore she shouldn't decide how to respond to needy children *only* because of what she feels.

CHILDREN OF GOD

On the other hand, it's equally dangerous to hold all emotional responses suspect. We are not Vulcans like *Star Trek's* Mr. Spock who acted out of logic and not feelings because his father was from a planet where the population was devoid of emotion.

We are children of Jehovah God who loves and mourns and who is called the "Father" or originator of compassion (2 Cor. 1:3).

Lynda's revulsion became profound sorrow and moved her to insist that she must have a transfer from the exam room where she had to help with abortions. Of course, our feelings can also motivate us to make wrong choices. Fear caused Peter to deny Christ and Abraham to pass off his wife as his sister—both definitely immoral acts.

Their fear wasn't wrong; the way they chose to act on their fear was.

So we can use our emotions most effectively, we need to ask ourselves, "What kind of emotional nature do I have?" Am I overinfluenced by the way I feel? Or have I shut off my feelings because I'm afraid they're not trustworthy? Am I too quick to act solely on the way I feel instead of calling my other faculties into play? If we know ourselves, we can take that information into account.

Used correctly, emotions will do what they're meant to do: motivate us to moral action. That's what they did for Jesus Christ. Anger moved Him to cleanse the temple.

Compassion frequently moved Him, as Gospel writers indicate (Matt. 9:36). When crowds came and stayed three days without eating, Jesus told His disciples, "I have compassion for these people. . . . I do not want to send them away hungry."

What followed was the miracle of the loaves and fishes

(15:32). It provided Him with the impetus and is meant to do the same for us.

Will is the power to choose. It would do us no good to formulate a biblical ethic on an issue if we were without the capacity to choose a stand and act on it. Like the rest of our human faculties, though, the ability to choose wisely and act on that choice must be cultivated.

"Making choices was the hardest thing I had to do," Jean told me. "I was very dependent. That's because I went from living at home in obedience to my mother to a husband who made the decisions. I liked it that way. I didn't want opinions of my own."

Then her husband founded a Christian organization, and she began to work with him. "My contact with misery in Third World countries prodded me to form personal values. A trip to our organization's work in Mexico City's largest garbage dump where people actually live in shacks and comb the garbage for food and things to sell was one experience that did that for me.

"Since then, I'm more aware of what I have. And I'm beginning to scale down my possessions. Not that I live shabbily; I don't. I still have more than some and at times I'm ashamed of it. But I'm learning to get along on less. Having things just isn't as important anymore."

Another change is in the area of work. "I was on a plane returning home when it hit me: *I am doing exactly what God wants me to do.* If I wasn't out raising funds, others wouldn't be able to go out and touch lives. To have that kind of personal conviction was another milestone."

As a younger Christian, I also brought some of the same unhealthy ideas about my will into my Christian life. Only I put a spiritual twist on the subject. "God doesn't want me to use my will. He wants me to let Him superimpose His will on me."

GOD GIVES US A WILL

When I embraced a more biblical view of who I was created to be, I realized that God had gifted me with the ability to choose and He meant for me to exercise it—to choose *His* will. Doing so was part of the process of becoming fully human.

My friend Evie is my alter ego. She has *no* trouble deciding what's right and setting her will to follow that course. When she decided she was charging too many purchases, she cut up her credit cards. When she decided a lottery was an unhealthy way for her state to collect revenue, she did not buy tickets.

But Evie has another problem: she is so strong-willed that she has to keep herself in check. She knows it would be easy for her to decide *for* God what His will is.

The woman who is timid about using her will becomes more facile with practice. That happened when I made a series of small moral choices: to take back the extra change a store clerk gave me; to change the subject when an acquaintance gossips. On the other hand, the strong-willed woman has to take special effort to rein herself in and pray, wait, and listen when forming a conviction.

God is just as pleased when we use our will to decide and act on what we believe is right as He was sorrowed when Eve chose wrongly. For we are exercising the gift of human choice—one of the greatest of all expressions of His love.

Spirit. When it's spelled with a small "s," it's the human dimension that enables us to know God relationally. Spelled with a capital "S," it's the person of God Himself.

The moment a woman invites Jesus Christ to be her Savior, God's Holy Spirit indwells her human spirit. She becomes one with Him. As a result, she knows God personally and has the capacity to sense His thoughts about life as she lives it.

"No one can know God's thoughts except God's own Spirit. And God has actually given us His Spirit" (1 Cor. 2:11-12, TLB).

As soon as we become His, God is ready to superintend our decision-making center. "When He, the Spirit of Truth, comes, He will guide you into all truth" (John 16:13).

Our part is first to *ask* Him to do that and mean it. Second, it's to cultivate our inner ability to sense the silent, inner voice by which He guides us "into all truth." Most often, He doesn't guide through a Damascus Road light from heaven flashed around us. It's in our spiritual dimension, through an inner *knowing* as He enlightens the eyes of our heart (Eph. 1:18). Learning to rest in His presence so we're quiet within is invaluable. Then, when He does illuminate a Scripture passage, we'll know it.

The more we live in unbroken fellowship with our Lord, the more spiritual our mind, conscience, emotion, and will become, and the more likely it will be that our choices reflect God's nature.

"It is the Holy Spirit who renders [the believer] spiritual. The meaning of spiritual is to belong to the Holy Spirit. He strengthens with might the human spirit so as to govern the entire man," writes Watchman Nee[6] (brackets added).

That, after all, is our goal.

1. *Walt Disney's Winnie the Pooh and Tigger Too* (New York: Random House, 1975).
2. R.E. Morosco, "Beyond Knee Jerk Thinking," *Eternity*, February 1983, p. 30.
3. Lauren Littauer Briggs, *What You Can Say . . . When You Don't Know What to Say* (Eugene, Ore.: Harvest House, 1985), p. 45.
4. Milton L. Rudnick, *Christian Ethics for Today* (Grand Rapids: Baker Book House, 1979), p. 124.
5. Garry Friesen with J. Robin Maxson, *Decision Making and the Will of God* (Portland, Ore.: Multnomah Press, 1980), p. 409.
6. Watchman Nee, *The Spiritual Life*, Vol. 2 (New York: Christian Fellowship Publishers, Inc., 1968), p. 18.

Five Key Principles

FIVE ❧

*F*ear prickled my insides as my husband, John, sagged onto the sofa. I sensed that this wasn't going to be an ordinary, "How was your day? Mine was busy, all right," exchange.

As John spoke, I could hear the pain behind every word. "I don't know if I can keep working at the TV station."

Recently, after a long period of unemployment, he'd taken a position as operations manager with a new television station. Now he had learned that they'd be using R-rated movies and "adult" programming to get a larger share of the pay-TV pie.

He didn't have the power to change the programming. Neither did he have to preview the shows himself, but could order someone else to do it. Still, the films came addressed to him. So to outsiders it would seem as though he was endorsing them.

The idea of him quitting his job for *any* reason terrified me. Having grown up poor, I felt secure only if I knew that we'd have a paycheck each month. Though I supplemented our income, it wasn't nearly enough to provide for us. Besides, John was fifty-six years old. How could he find another position at his age?

TALKED TOGETHER

We talked about it together, the way we did about every major decision. Sure, it was *his* job and *his* choice, but in our marriage we'd always been partners. The following weeks, we both prayed about whether or not he should resign.

Evenings as we sat on the sofa with Puppy in her basket at our feet, we reviewed the questions:

"Should he resign his position because of R- and X-rated programming?" It was socially acceptable to do what he was doing.

"Was he, as an employee, only responsible to obey orders?"

"Was he absolved because he didn't have to review the films himself?"

"Did he want to quit because he didn't like the job and was only using the moral issue as an excuse?"

"Did he have the right to expose his wife and children to financial insecurity?" He had no retirement plan.

This was not the first time we'd had to make such a decision. Twenty-five years before—right after we became Christians—he was traffic manager for an aluminum corporation. In that position he was expected to lie about delivery dates. "Sure, your shipment's on the way," even though he knew it was still in the warehouse. When he became a Christian, the lies stuck in his throat.

That time, we'd prayed separately for guidance and before

long agreed that he must resign. He did.

But deciding to do that was easier at thirty than at fifty-six. I needed concrete biblical principles to stand on so that if John resigned and no new job appeared and money ran out, I'd still *know. We obeyed the truth.*

KEY PRINCIPLES

The New Testament does provide ready-made, key principles that provide moral guidance in situations like these. Five that are specifically stated are these:

1. Salt and light
2. The Golden Rule
3. Liberty
4. The weaker brother/sister
5. Love

Each key principle is a summary of teachings on a particular subject. Like all principles, they can be applied to a broad spectrum of situations. Not that they are *Reader's Digest* condensations of the Bible for those who have neither the time nor the inclination to read the whole Book — *My Gospel is the Golden Rule.* They are central truths reduced to their essence by a God who knows that's what we need.

Salt and Light. These two concepts are part of Jesus' Sermon on the Mount. "You are the salt of the earth" (Matt. 5:13). "You are the light of the world" (v. 14).

He had just explained that the most blessed or happy people are, for example, the ones who recognize their poverty of spirit, show mercy, are pure in heart, and are peacemakers (vv. 1-10). He went on to intimate that men and women who live like this are like salt and light in the world.

Why salt? It's a substance that creates a thirst and preserves against decay. The Christian "is a check, a control, an antiseptic in society," explains D. Martyn Lloyd-Jones.[1]

Light exposes dirt and grime the way a sudden burst of full sun reveals dust and cobwebs safely hidden on a gray day. It cannot do otherwise.

"A man truly living and functioning as a Christian will stand out. He will be like salt . . . like . . . a candle set upon a candlestick. If we do what's natural for us because we are partakers of the life of God, we will reveal dirt and grime and make people thirsty for righteousness."[2]

So when we face a moral choice, we're to ask ourselves: "Is this an opportunity to be salt and light?" That's what someone close to me had to ask herself when she went to audition for a part in *Candide*.

"I hadn't read the script, but when I saw the content, I felt that it was too risqué for me to be associated with. So I told the director I was leaving the audition and told him why."

The Golden Rule. "In everything, do to others what you would have them do to you, for this sums up the Law and the Prophets" (Matt. 7:12). This principle expands on what came before. In this case, it's Jesus' previous statement about judging others in verses 1-6; the words that follow about prayer in verses 7-11 are parenthetical.

What He was saying is this: *Instead of judging others uncharitably, put yourself in their place.* That's what I had to do when I worked as a salesclerk and was told to sell products as "fresh" that in my opinion, certainly were not. *Would I want to spend my money for products like these?*

Since my answer was an absolute no, I began to pray about what to do. Before I got around to confronting my supervisor, I was given permission to decide when these products' shelf life was over and to pull them when it was. Had God *not* intervened, I would have had to speak up and pay the consequences.

Liberty. "So Christ has made us free. Now make sure that

you stay free" (Gal. 5:1, TLB). Under the Old Testament agreement, morals had been carefully legislated. In addition to the Ten Commandments, God gave specific instructions for specific areas of an Israelite's life—from purification after childbirth to a woman's conduct during menstruation.

Those civil, social, dietary, and relational laws do not apply to Christians. When a thing is neither commanded nor forbidden in the Bible, says Merrill Unger, "Christian liberty may be exercised and should be allowed."³ We have the freedom to decide for ourselves—not so we'll be able to live on the moral edge—but so we'll take the initiative to choose personal morality and live out of it.

But many women I've talked with say that they were raised believing that they were supposed to adhere to a list of "do's" and "don'ts." "My parents and my church had a very strict list of things that were wrong, like wearing makeup, going to movies, playing cards, and cutting my hair. Until I was much older, I never knew I had the liberty to decide such things for myself."

The woman who decided not to try out for *Candide* says, "When I first became a Christian I was impressed with the idea that it was wrong to drink anything with alcohol. As the years passed, I came to believe that was a cultural standard I had picked up from other Christians. Eventually I added the occasional glass of wine or beer to the menu . . . feeling that I'm free to do so."

So we won't use it indiscriminately, in Scripture the Law of Liberty is partnered with another key principle.

The Weaker Brother/Sister. "Be careful, however, that the exercise of your freedom does not become a stumbling block to the weak" (1 Cor. 8:9). The problem in Bible days wasn't whether or not to watch the latest scorching miniseries or to work in a store that sells *Hustler*, but whether or not to eat meat that had been sacrificed to idols (Rom. 14:1-15). Usually, the Greeks and Romans burned some of a sacrifice as part of their heathen religious ritual and saved the tastier cuts to serve at a banquet. The rest was sold in the marketplace.

Some Christians, like Paul, agreed that sacrificing an animal to a god that doesn't even exist can't make the roast that comes from it evil. But for others, to eat it for Sunday dinner or at a neighborhood potluck was sinful.

So here's the general guideline that Paul gave. "No food is unclean in itself. But if anyone regards something as unclean, then for him it is unclean. If your brother is distressed because of what you eat, you are no longer acting in love" (vv. 14-15). To influence someone to act against their conscience is to do them serious harm.

A writer friend would like to serve wine at family dinners, but never does because one of her grown children is an alcoholic. To do so would not only be a stumbling block to her offspring, it would also seem to give the individual permission to drink.

When we do refrain from something in which we feel we have liberty, it's not our convictions we're changing, only our behavior, Walvoord and Zuck remind us. And we're doing it because we might influence a less knowledgeable Christian (or one who perceives biblical guidelines differently) to go against his conscience.

That's a whole lot different than trying to defer to every person's peculiarities. "Every Sunday when I was a teenager, an older woman picked me up and drove me to church," a friend recalled. "Every Sunday, she let me know that she disapproved of the fact that I wore lipstick."

The older woman wasn't a weaker sister, only a critical one who made a practice of judging harshly anyone who failed to agree with her point of view. "Pharisees," Garry Friesen calls such legalistic people. "He *takes offense* when no offense is given. . . . The Pharisee is *a professing believer with strong con-*

victions who, because of his own pride, takes offense at those who resist his pressure to conform to his point of view.[4]

What question should we ask ourselves when deciding whether to curb our liberty because of a weaker brother/sister? "Is this an action which Scripture neither commands nor forbids but that could influence someone to act against his conscience?" That's the criteria John and I used when deciding early in our Christian lives whether or not to drink alcohol. Friends in the church drank in moderation, but the custodian — a young man who'd recently become our friend — had a drinking problem. There was no question about it: if we used alcohol, he could easily use the fact as an excuse to go against his better judgment. And he simply could not drink.

Love. An expert in the law asked Jesus what was the greatest commandment.

"Jesus replied: 'Love the Lord your God with all your heart and with all your soul and with all your mind. This is the first and greatest commandment. And the second is like it: Love your neighbor as yourself' " (Matt. 22:37). This key principle is no warm, fuzzy formula — *if I just think lovingly, whatever I do will be OK.* Nor is it the kind of love popularized by situational ethics that bends like Gumby to suit the occasion.

The love described here is *agapao* — completely unselfish and self-sacrificing. Jesus Christ provided a perspective on its dimensions. It always performs the greatest good for the recipient. Never, for example, does He use it as a cloak for goalongism, to avoid confrontation.

How can we turn this general principle into a specific to help us know what to do *now?*

1. Ask ourselves: "Which choice will show the most *agape* love for God and the people involved?" The choices may seem to be in opposition. They did at first for me. If John kept his job, wouldn't he be showing love to his family by supporting us? At the same time, I knew that he'd be dishon-

oring God by seeming to endorse erotic programming.

But would he *really* be showing *agape* love for his sons and me by compromising his ethics? Of course not. If he did, he'd be teaching that it's OK to compromise with evil in order to survive.

Dodie had a hard time trying to decide what the most loving action would be when her homosexual son wanted to come for a visit and bring his lover. "The practice of homosexuality is against everything I believe in. But I don't want to alienate my son. How can I influence him for God if I do that?"

She finally decided to tell her son that he and his live-in homosexual partner could come. "But you'll have to have separate bedrooms." They both knew what her convictions about practicing homosexuality were. The most loving thing she could do, she decided, was to stand firm. She couldn't control his behavior outside her home, but she could while he was there. In doing so, she'd be showing love for God by being obedient to Him, and for her son by confronting him with the wrongness of his lifestyle while she lovingly accepted him as a person.

My husband made his own moral choice one morning after several weeks of prayer and reflection on key biblical principles. He handed in his resignation. In it he said he was leaving because of his personal standards and that his convictions made the station's programming unacceptable to him.

It's been more than ten years since John made that decision. His stand about "adult" programming closed many doors to him in secular television. Did we ever regret our choice? No, not the choice itself. For us at least, it was the right one. But when money was scarce and our emotions were frayed, like the time I had cancer and we had no health insurance, we did wonder whether God would keep supplying our needs.

Of course, He always did. Now, retrospectively, I can honestly say that we were privileged to have been given such an opportunity to be, in however small a way, salt and light.

1. D. Martyn Lloyd-Jones, *Studies in the Sermon on the Mount*, Vol. I (London: Inter-Varsity Fellowship, 1960), p. 158.
2. Ibid., p. 174.
3. Merrill F. Unger, *Unger's Bible Dictionary* (Chicago: Moody Press, 1961), p. 660.
4. Garry Friesen with J. Robin Maxson, *Decision Making and the Will of God* (Portland, Ore.: Multnomah Press, 1980), p. 409.

Forming More Principles

SIX ❦

Three experiences compelled me to keep searching until I discovered a way to resolve personal moral dilemmas. There were, of course, the issues themselves that kept nagging at me. *Should I keep investing time and money in nursing home residents? Should I adopt the stand against dancing and other recreational issues that I've been taught or not? How do I feel about abortion in the case of rape or incest?*

Experience #1 provided me with the church's permission to decide for myself. Not long after my husband and I left the mission with which we'd been affiliated, we attended an adult Sunday School class in our new church. I caught my breath in disbelief when the thoughtful-looking man who led the class asked *what we thought about capital punishment.* We read Scriptures, and he asked *how we thought they applied to that subject.* He asked *us to explain the logic behind our stand.*

ONE RIGHT WAY?

No one suggested that there was only one right way for Christians to think about that issue—or the other issues we discussed. Instead, we were strongly encouraged to investigate issues and think them through for ourselves. It stunned me to think that a large church in a well-respected evangelical denomination endorsed such liberty.

Experience #2 had convinced me that women needed such a plan. I invited a group of writer friends to my home to discuss contemporary issues. How would we decide what to do if our teenage daughter was pregnant? If she was sexually active and no amount of talking made her stop? Would we make sure she had access to birth control?

We sipped tea and talked and sipped tea and talked until someone said she absolutely had to get home. "So what have we concluded?" I wanted to know.

"Deciding about these things is *hard* because I don't know how to go about it. I guess I'd just do what I felt was right and count on the fact that God knew I'd done the best I could," one of the more vocal women present sighed. The rest nodded in agreement.

After they left, I picked up teacups and straightened the living room and gathered loose ends of the evening's conversation . . . "Don't know . . . how do we decide? . . . " I slid between the covers and perplexity slid in alongside me. Before the day fogged by sleep, I looked silently to God for the hint of a trail through the woods.

Experience #3 convinced me that I could formulate such a plan for women. One afternoon as I searched the public library shelves for help, I found *Christian Ethics for Today: An Evangelical Approach* by Milton L. Rudnick.

"In this book I present directly and unequivocally the approach which to me best seems to express what Scripture and evangelical theology teach about knowing and doing what is right. Then I plug these elements into a problem-solving process which facilitates their application to daily life."[1]

Rudnick showed me that there was a process and provided one he'd worked out. But I wanted to help ordinary women like me who lived on Maple Avenue in suburbia, in a metropolitan highrise or at the end of a country lane form a personal value system. It needed to take into account the fact that many of us have been dependent on others to decide for us, so we approach the idea tenuously.

We also need a plan to help us know how to decide about the particular issues with which we, as females, must wrestle. So I prayed and read down the library shelves and researched and interviewed. All the while, I used what I was learning to make my own moral choices.

I COULD BE WRONG

It was especially difficult for me to deduce principles from Scripture. That's because I was a literalist. Instructions had to be spelled out precisely. I dared not risk drawing conclusions. *I could be wrong.*

I studied the Bible the same way—*Show me chapter and verse so I'll know what to do.* Forming biblical principles simply took too much original thinking.

One of my canning failures during those days shows what I mean. It was late summer, and I decided to make sweet pickles to please my husband. Religiously I tried to follow my neighbor's recipe. *Pour boiling water over the cucumbers for three days. Pour boiling syrup over them on the fourth day.*

What went wrong I'm not sure. I think I failed to drain off the water before I poured in the syrup. The directions didn't *say* to do that. Anyway, my pickles were green mush.

These days I'd think with more initiative. *It makes sense to pour off the water first, even if it doesn't say so in the recipe.*

I'm not the woman now that I was then. More confidence in myself as a person has given me more confidence in my decision-making center. Gradually I've learned to use those God-given abilities to deduce principles. But it's because of my own ineptness that I say to you with confidence: no matter how inept you may feel, *you can do it too.*

Of all the study skills I've acquired since I became a Christian, learning to form biblical principles has been one of the most valuable. It has reduced a complexity of teachings scattered from Genesis to Revelation to "take-alongs" that I can hold in my mind and apply.

That's true because, as I've said, a principle is a guideline or a summary statement. It's a fundamental truth on which others are based. "Love God . . . love man . . . " is a plain statement that summarizes many biblical teachings. It's a key principle on which to form a plethora of other guidelines — from how to relate to a son who practices homosexual acts to whether or not to regularly fix food forbidden for health reasons for a mate who demands it. Regarding the son: *Love doesn't compromise with truth.* Regarding a wife toward her husband: *Love acts constructively.*

STEPS FOR FORMULATING PRINCIPLES

How can we be sure that we won't wander into theological left field when we formulate our own principles? By taking some simple steps.

1. Find out what the passage we're considering really means. Recently a friend said she knew it was wrong to desire things and based her statement on Psalm 23:1: "I shall not want."

After we talked, she came to see that's not what the psalm-ist meant at all. The word translated "want" in the *King James Version* has more than one meaning in English. The appropri-ate one here is brought out in the *New International Version* as well as the *Amplified Bible*. "I shall lack nothing," and "I shall not lack."

So look up words of which you are uncertain in an English dictionary. Check alternate meanings. Read the passage in a couple of other translations of the Bible. If necessary, consult a dictionary of New Testament words. Decide which meaning is appropriate. You'll be more apt to base your principles on the real meaning of the passage.

Theologian R.C. Sproul provides a good rule of thumb. "I believe the Bible is uniquely inspired and infallible. . . . But for matters of interpretation the Bible does not take on some special magic that changes basic literary patterns of inter-pretation. . . . A verb is a verb and a noun is a noun."[2]

2. Consider the context. It's as dangerous to take a sen-tence out of a sermon, parable, or psalm as it is to read only one statement in a letter from cousin Mattie describing her new will. To understand the key principles of salt and light described in Matthew 5, we must read the Beatitudes that precede it. To understand the principle of the weaker brother/sister and the law of liberty, we must read all Paul has to say on the subject in 1 Corinthians 8–10.

Decide where in the chapter the subject begins and where it ends and read the entire segment. Often, reading all the text under a subhead is a good idea, like "Jesus Heals a Man Born Blind" in John 9:1-12. Other times, you may need to read more than that.

3. Investigate the cultural situation. Was the passage writ-ten to straighten out some problem in the early church? I had to decide whether or not a woman is allowed to teach men because I was being asked to address mixed groups. Besides, I

wrote books and articles for both sexes.

When I read, "Women should remain silent in the churches" (1 Cor. 14:34), I asked myself if Paul was writing to correct a particular situation that existed then or not. It seemed to me that he was. To be sure, I checked a reliable reference book.

"Certain women were troublesome in the church at Ephesus (1 Tim. 5:11-15; 2 Tim. 3:6-9) and they appear to have been a major part of the cause of the false teachers making headway there."[3]

Women were teaching and prophesying in other places so it's likely that in 1 Corinthians 14:34 Paul was addressing a particular situation. I wasn't being troublesome, only exercising my gift of teaching. So this passage wasn't one I could use to form a principle on which to base my decision. I'd keep on researching Scripture to see what it had to say about women teaching.

Some passages that were written to address a New Testament problem do also contain overriding truths that apply generally today. Take the subject of the weaker brother/sister. Even though the subject is sacrificing meat to idols which most of us don't do, Paul's key principle — *Don't be a stumbling block* — does apply today. That's because we face different kinds of situations that can have the same result. We can influence someone to go against a genuine conviction.

"My sister believes it's wrong to watch movies because she says she'd be endorsing a corrupt industry. I believe that many industries have the taint of evil. Lots of periodicals advertise cigarettes, for instance, but we still buy them.

"To my way of thinking, films are neither good nor evil in themselves and it's OK to watch good ones. But when my sister's visiting we don't rent videos. Not only would it cause a rift between us, but she might be tempted to go against her conscience. I think she'd have to be convinced first that it's OK for her to watch."

So if you suspect the passage you're reading does address a first-century cultural situation, ask yourself if a parallel situation exists today. Is there a basic truth that applies now? If you need background information, look in a Bible commentary.

REDUCE TEACHINGS TO A PRINCIPLE

With those precautions in mind, how do we go about reducing a group of teachings to a principle? It's easier if you remember two things.

1. Principles are simple, general statements that you can use as moral guidelines. "Do to others what you would have them do to you" (Matt. 7:12). Your principles should be the same kind of simple, general statements. They may be the words of the Scripture itself or a summary statement in your own words.

2. Your principle will embody the primary teaching of the passage. Paul's description of the fruit of the Spirit (Gal. 5:22-23) is part of a unit of thought that begins in verse 16 and ends in verse 26. Look it over and see if you agree that the principle could be, "Christians are to be guided by the Holy Spirit" (vv. 16-26).

To see how the process works, let's look at three familiar passages: The Twenty-third Psalm, The Parable of the Good Samaritan, and the Love Chapter.

The Twenty-third Psalm. In this lyric, David compares God's care of His people to a shepherd's care of his sheep. Because "The Lord is my shepherd, I shall lack nothing," God's provisions include green pastures, quiet waters, inner restoration, and companionship through valleys. His sheep can count on goodness and love throughout their lives and a home in heaven for eternity.

1. What is the subject of the psalm?
God's care.
2. What fundamental truth does the passage teach?
God cares for believers the way a shepherd cares for his sheep.
The Parable of the Good Samaritan (Luke 10:25-37). This story of Jesus' is His answer to a Jewish lawkeeper's question, "What must I do to inherit eternal life?" First, the Lord asks the lawkeeper what he thinks is the Bible's answer to that question.

"Love the Lord your God. . . . Love your neighbor as yourself," the man shot back.

Immediately, though, he felt caught in the condemning vice of his own words. He had not loved his neighbor. So, looking for escape, he asked another question. "And who is my neighbor?"

Jesus told the story of a traveler who'd been beaten and robbed and left half dead on the road from Jerusalem to Jericho. A priest and a Levite (both religious Jews) deliberately ignored the individual. But a Samaritan, a natural enemy of the Jews, went out of his way to care for the man.

" 'Which of these three do you think was a neighbor to the man who fell into the hands of robbers?'

"The expert in the law replied, 'The one who had mercy on him.'

"Jesus told him, 'Go and do likewise.' "

The subject of the story? *Neighborliness.* The main teaching reduced to a general statement? *Be the kind of neighbor who shows love even to your enemies.*

The Love Chapter (1 Cor. 13). After discussing particular gifts that the Holy Spirit gives Christians, Paul describes the greatest gift: love. No matter what else we may be able to do, if we aren't innately loving, we have accomplished little.

He describes the facets of love: patience, kindness, generosity, thoughtfulness, humility, good-temperedness, hopefulness, perseverance. Love is important because it alone will endure and because it is a symbol of maturity.

The subject of the story? *Love.* The main teaching reduced to a general statement? *Unselfish love surpasses all spiritual gifts.*

Hone your ability to deduce principles during your daily Bible reading. Ask yourself: 1. "What is the main subject?" 2. "What statement sums up the main teaching?" Record your conclusions.

In the next chapter, we'll learn to form biblical principles to guide us in making moral choices.

1. Milton L. Rudnick, *Christian Ethics for Today* (Grand Rapids: Baker Book House, 1979), p. 16.
2. R.C. Sproul, *Knowing Scripture* (Downers Grove, Ill.: InterVarsity Press, 1977), p. 63.
3. Gordon D. Fee and Douglas Stuart, *How to Read the Bible for All It's Worth* (Grand Rapids: Zondervan Publishing Co., 1982), p. 69.

The Decision-Making Process (1)

SEVEN ❦

Y
ou've just learned that your son's school is considering the distribution of condoms. *What should my stand be on that?* You decide to investigate the subject soon.

An hour later you remember the dessert you promised for Gourmet Club meeting. The phone rings and before you know it you've lost an hour talking to a friend about what she did and you did over the weekend. You remember that you'll have no free time tomorrow because you're going to hit the garage sales.

I'm just too busy to explore the condom issue now. My gut feeling is to oppose it. But what about kids who are having sex and are in danger of getting AIDS? At least condoms lower the risk. . . . I'll just pray about it and count on God to show me what to do.

There are times when we have to decide that way out of

necessity, but is this really one of them? Or are we playing Peter Pan?

Let me major in minors. Please don't ask me to assume the responsibility of Christian womanhood.

I sensed that Glenna wanted to abdicate her responsibility. "I married because I was pregnant. Life at home was pretty awful, and I thought that this man was my ticket out. It didn't take very long for me to find out that I didn't love my husband.

"We've been married five years and I'm miserable. I know it's partly because of the baggage I brought with me due to childhood experiences. I'm getting counseling but my husband isn't interested in going."

I heard from Glenna a few months later. She'd filed for divorce and it would be final soon. Had she taken time to study Scripture on the subject?

"Not seriously," she admitted. "I just had to get out of the marriage."

I understood. You probably do too. There have been times when both you and I have acted simply because we wanted the situation to be over.

But we are called to obey our higher sense. Hers is the voice to which we must listen. Hers is the voice calling us to greater maturity.

Which moral dilemma do we decide about first? Usually, life decides for us. We face a crisis and have to know what is the moral action.

It may be how to decide what television shows the family should watch because we've passed through the living room and heard dialogue that made us recoil—again. Or whether or not to go along with some of the acts our husbands want us to perform when we have sex. We could go on ignoring the situation, but we don't want to do that. We want our own moral point of view.

FIRST WE PRAY

First, of course, we pray. That doesn't merely mean asking God to guide our thoughts. Certainly He will do that. "The Spirit of truth . . . will guide you into all truth" (John 16:13).

The Holy Spirit is our Counselor (John 14:16-18). He's here—in us—and one of the reasons He came is to participate in our entire decision-making process. So, instead of a prayer at the start and a thank-You at the finish, we can think our thoughts to Him throughout, listen for His perspective and warnings; ask expectantly for Him to lead us to sources of information.

It's important that we be sure at the outset that there's not a sin in our lives around which we're stepping gingerly like a pile of garbage. We must ask God to search us, then wait and listen and confess and be forgiven if necessary.

Like us, first-century Gentile Christians had to struggle hard to form convictions that reflected the character of God. A main reason for them was that they were caught between legalists and pagans. Did they make their moral choices based on old pagan values? Should they accept the ideas of Jewish legalists, or should they use a new value system? If so, what was it?

Paul prayed for those first-century Christians, and we can use his words to pray for ourselves.

1. Ask for "the Spirit of wisdom and revelation, so that you may know Him better" (Eph. 1:17). That's insight into the issue before us and a fresh glimpse of Christ's nature.

2. Request that "the eyes of your heart may be enlightened in order that you may know the hope to which He has called you" (v. 18). That's Christlikeness. You're asking to make the kind of moral choice that He'd make.

3. Tell Him that you're going to count on "His incomparably great power for us who believe" (v. 19). What power is

that? "His mighty strength, which He exerted in Christ when He raised Him from the dead" (vv. 19-20). As my grandson says, "That's awesome!"

You're faced with a specific problem that's kept you staring into space during your coffee breaks. It seems that your husband wants to buy a pleasure boat and your son is griping because everyone but him has designer jeans. You have to admit that you're dissatisfied with the same old living room furniture and would love to redecorate.

"How *should* Christians spend their money anyway?" you keep asking yourself as you run your finger around the rim of your coffee cup. "Is it right to buy a new sofa and a new boat when people die of starvation every day? Is there a certain standard of living that God wants Christians to adopt? How do I know what's need and what's luxury?"

If you're single, the question may be, "Is it right for me to buy the luxury sports car I've dreamed of? Or should I go for an economy model and give the money saved to worthy causes?"

PRAY SPECIFICALLY

You pray specifically for wisdom and enlightenment and for God to demonstrate His power by showing the truth about stewardship and materialism.

Exactly what question is it to which you need to find an answer? Phrase it specifically so that it expresses the problem you actually face.

"Should we spend money on a boat, designer jeans, and redecorating the living room?" "Should I buy the sports car?" Record the question in your journal, notebook, on your computer, or on tape.

"Beneath every moral question that we have to answer

there are additional, deeper questions. These questions beneath the questions are usually called "moral issues."[1]

Brainstorm ones that come to mind. "Are we being materialistic by spending money on things that aren't essential? Is there a criteria Christians should use when deciding about luxury expenditures? What is materialism anyway? What makes a Christian a good steward? What's the difference between necessities and luxuries? When does spending get out of hand?"

Or suppose your dilemma has to do with artificial insemination. A physician has said that the only way you can have children is to be artificially inseminated with sperm by a donor since your husband is infertile. You ask yourself: "Should I try to have a baby through artificial insemination with donor sperm?" It's not only infertile marrieds that are asking themselves that question: child-hungry singles are too.

Some of the moral questions that grow out of that one are: "Is artificial insemination right or wrong? Would I be circumventing the will of God? Is it moral to conceive artificially when there are adoptable children who need homes? Is artificial insemination by a donor the same as committing adultery?"

Several women I know had to decide about rock music because it was blasting from the stereos in their sons'/daughters' rooms. "Should I let my child listen to and/or perform rock music?" The questions behind the question? "Are some kinds of rock music moral and some not? Is Christian rock always acceptable? Can music as well as lyrics be immoral? Do I need to know the personal morality of the performer?" Or you may be asking yourself whether or not it's acceptable to listen to the kind of music you loved in pre-Jesus days.

Next, brainstorm and put down all your thoughts on the

subject. Don't ignore ones that seem ridiculous or make you feel guilty.

POSSESSIONS

If the subject is money, your thinking might run this way: "Jerry's a Christian but he does tend to want expensive toys. That bothers me—first because I'm not sure we can really afford them, and second because it's one more sign that money and what it can buy are too important to him. A desire for designer jeans bothers me because it's a sign that our son is preoccupied with status.

"I'm afraid that possessions mean too much to me too. That we've all missed the mark. That God doesn't want us to be concerned with these things. Maybe I am too preoccupied with what people think. Besides, my mother lets me know that she doesn't approve of the way I spend my money. Is she right? Whenever I hear a sermon on stewardship or when I hear about someone giving self-sacrificially, I feel guilty. Should I feel that way?"

Now that you know precisely what your questions are and what you're thinking on the subject, it's time to start looking for answers in God's Word.

To do that you'll need the following books:

● A Bible with a subject index—not just a concordance.

● At least two translations of the Bible. Choose ones recognized for their accuracy. One should be a paraphrase in modern English.

● An English dictionary

If you want to purchase some of these and aren't sure which volumes are best, ask your pastor, other church staff member, or a mature Christian friend for recommendations.

Other reference books you may need include the following.

You may not own them but they're probably available in your church library, public library, or a local Bible school or seminary library. Or perhaps your pastor or a friend will let you use theirs.

- A Bible dictionary to find additional information on a particular subject.
- A Bible commentary or two. Be sure they're written by scholars who are doctrinally sound.
- A dictionary of Bible words that gives additional information about their meaning, like *Vine's Expository Dictionary of Old and New Testament Words* (W.E. Vine, Old Testament Studies edited by F.F. Bruce, Fleming H. Revell).
- A concordance that lists all the references for a particular word and gives the Hebrew or Greek definition, like the one compiled by James Strong.

For the next step—finding biblical principles from which you'll deduce God's perspective—make a good-sized block of time available so you won't have one eye on the clock. First review key principles like the ones in chapter 5. Do any apply to your subject?

For example, you may ask yourself, "Does Jesus' call to be salt and light have anything to do with my view of money?" *The way I spend money as well as my attitude toward possessions shows the importance I place on these things.*

ARTIFICIAL INSEMINATION

How about key principles as they pertain to artificial insemination? "Does the law of liberty have anything to do with it?" *Since artificial insemination is neither commanded nor forbidden in the Bible, I have liberty to decide about it for myself.* To know how to decide, you'll look for other biblical passages to guide you in your choice.

Start by listing key words that come to mind. For your decision about whether or not to buy luxuries, the words that come to mind first are *money and stewardship*. For artificial insemination, some of those words are *children, childlessness, reproduction, adultery, immorality*. Not every subject (reproduction is one possibility) will be listed.

Of the passages listed under "children," some won't apply. Several do state plainly or imply that *children are a gift from God*, so that's the principle you record (Gen. 33:5; 48:9; Ps. 127:3, 5). *Childlessness*, you learn from the references listed under that heading, *is sorrowful*, so you record that as well.

Adultery, you know, is definitely forbidden (Ex. 20:14). *But do I believe that artificial insemination by donor is the same as adultery?* You review the definition of "adultery" in *Webster's New World Dictionary, Second College Edition*. "Voluntary sexual intercourse between a married man and a woman not his wife, or between a married woman and a man not her husband."

You phrase that commandment as a positive statement: *Have sexual intercourse only with your husband.* Since a physician implants donor sperm at the time of ovulation, you know you wouldn't actually have intercourse. This knowledge alone doesn't satisfy you, though.

You discover that the word "intercourse" isn't in the Bible. Instead, the KJV uses "knew" and the NIV uses "lay with." (You find that out when you remember the passage in which Adam and Eve first have sex in Genesis and look it up.) There aren't many helpful references for "knew," "know," or "lay with" in your subject index or concordance, so you consult an exhaustive concordance.

One reference that particularly interests you is in the New Testament. "[Joseph] knew [Mary] not till she had brought forth her firstborn son: and he called His name Jesus" (Matt. 1:25, KJV, bracketed words mine). You look up "knew" and "know" in *Vine's Expository Dictionary*. It frequently indicates a relationship and conveys "the thought of connection or union as between man and woman."[2] *Sexual intercourse implies relationship* you record next.

Now you think of still another word—"conception." By looking up the word in your subject index, you find that, after childbearing years, Sarah became pregnant and bore Isaac because of God's intervention (Gen. 21:1-2). So did Rebekah, Isaac's wife, who was barren (25:21). Manoah's wife was also sterile and childless but God intervened in that situation as well (Jud. 13). Their son was Samson. But as you learned when you looked up "childlessness," God did not always intervene. "Michal daughter of Saul had no children to the day of her death" (2 Sam. 6:23).

Sometimes God chooses to overrule sterility; other times He does not.

MONEY

On the subject of money, you look in Ecclesiastes 5. Solomon, the author, says in the verses before that the poor suffer because of universal injustice. He also says, "He who loves money shall never have enough. The foolishness of thinking that wealth brings happiness! The more you have, the more you spend, right up to the limits of your income" (vv. 10-11, TLB).

How to summarize the passage in a simple statement? "Money doesn't bring happiness."

Another reference under "money" is 1 Timothy 6:10. Since Timothy is a letter written for the purpose of teaching, it holds special importance as a guide. "For the love of money is the first step toward all kinds of sin" (TLB). The *Amplified Bible* helps you understand what "love" means. "It is through this *craving* that some have been led astray" (6:10, italics mine). We only crave money because it will buy things. It's possessions we crave. That ties in with what Solomon has to say.

Reading before and after verse 10, you find that Paul has been warning against false teachers whose motivation was greed. "We should be well satisfied without money if we have enough food and clothing" (v. 8, TLB).

Was Paul condemning those who lived anything less than a spartan lifestyle? When you read verses 17-19, you conclude that he wasn't. He doesn't condemn being rich but says wealthy people shouldn't trust in their money, but be ready to share with others what God has given them.

Using pencil and paper, you make several tries and discard them before you come up with a statement that says it best for you. "Craving for possessions leads away from God." You decide to write a second statement too based on verses 17-19. "Money is a gift from God meant to do good."

How much biblical research is enough? You're finished when you feel satisfied that you have a pretty good overview of what God has to say. Then it's time to draw conclusions based on the principles you've accumulated. You're on your way to forming a personal, *biblically* centered conviction.

1. Milton L. Rudnick, *Christian Ethics for Today* (Grand Rapids: Baker Book House, 1979), p. 77.
2. W.E. Vine, Old Testament Edited by F.F. Bruce, *Vine's Expository Dictionary of Old and New Testament Words* (Old Tappan, N.J.: Fleming H. Revell Co., 1981), p. 298.

The Decision-Making Process (2)

EIGHT ❦

*E*xactly how can you use the general biblical principles you've collected to help you decide whether or not to spend money on luxuries? By using your God-given deductive reasoning—your ability to draw conclusions and apply the general truths to your specific situation.

Practice sound thinking—not colored by what you want to be true, but solidly founded on what *is* true. Be sure to ask God to help you think straight and point out any deviations if they occur.

Follow these three steps to apply general principles in a specific way:

1. List the biblical principles you've formulated.
2. Personalize the principles.
3. Summarize your conclusions.

LIST BIBLICAL PRINCIPLES

I'll use the three on money as an example. Of course, if that were the subject you'd been working on, you'd have more than these.

"Money doesn't bring happiness."

"Craving for possessions leads away from God."

"Money is a gift from God meant to do good."

The idea isn't to come up with a theological treatise on money. Nor is it to write a paper to be graded by a seminary professor. Your conclusions need to be based, as nearly as you can make them, on the biblical truths and be simple and direct so they cut to the core of the matter. Of course, because we're human our decisions will be influenced by our particular personality. God understands that.

PERSONALIZE THE PRINCIPLES

If my son's jeans were up to his ankles and the rear ends were paper thin, I'd need help that was as specific as I could get it because I'd need to replace them *now*. Throughout the process, I'd need to remember that there *are* no absolutes on designer jeans. Nor are there any regarding boats and cars and new furniture. God expects me to come to a personal conclusion. Then my convictions about money and materialism in this area would become part of my personal value system. I'd think about the principles again, this time seeing how they apply to my particular situation. My thinking might go something like this—and I'd write my thoughts in my journal:

Money doesn't bring happiness. In this case, money stands for designer jeans. For my son to count on big-ticket jeans to make him feel good about himself is the wrong way to go. Craving for them leads away from God because he'd be trusting in a pair of pants and not in the fact that he's valuable because he's God's special creation.

He needs to have jeans that are sturdy, fit well, are stylish, and look good on him. To spend twice as much as we need to for the wrong reasons isn't good stewardship. Money is a gift from God to do good. It's not a birthright. Its primary purposes are, first, to meet our needs (needs include essentials — and I do believe relaxation and recreation are essentials). Second, it's meant to do good to others.

SUMMARIZE YOUR CONCLUSIONS

Make them as directly applicable to your situation as you can. I'd do it something like this:

a. Don't spend money on expensive items so we'll feel successful and as though we have status.

b. An expensive purchase isn't necessarily wrong. It's the motivation behind it that matters.

c. Keep focusing on God and let Him show us how to spend the money He allows us to have.

I'd check to be as sure as I could that my conclusions are based squarely on the biblical principles I've formed. Will they convince your son? Maybe not. But if he's desperate for expensive clothes to feel good about himself, his real problem isn't money. It's self-worth. You need to help him work through that. The same holds true for you and your new furniture or sports car.

How would you use deductive reasoning — part of your decision-making center — to draw sound conclusions about artificial insemination? By following the same steps.

1. *List the biblical principles you've formulated.* Children are a gift from God; childlessness is sorrowful; have sexual intercourse only with your husband; sexual intercourse implies

relationship; sometimes God chooses to overrule sterility, sometimes He does not.

2. *Personalize the principles.* Having children is not a right. They're a gift from God. He understands my sorrow over childlessness. Sexual intercourse, through which children are usually conceived, is to be only with my husband and is not an act but an expression of intimacy. I can ask God to remove my infertility, but whether He does or not is up to Him.

3. *Summarize your conclusions.*

a. Since having children is a gift and not a right, I am not to blame the gift-giver for my infertility.

b. I can express my sorrow to God; He understands.

c. I have liberty to decide whether or not I feel that artificial insemination by donor is intercourse or not, since it isn't stated in Scripture.

d. I have biblical precedent to pray to have a child by natural means, but I must accept the fact that the answer will be based on God's will and not mine.

Use the same three steps for any issue—from abortion to the rightness of sexual desire and the extent to which it can be freely expressed in marriage.

Now that you've personalized biblical principles, expand your perspective by exploring extrabiblical sources—both secular and Christian. They include books and articles on the subject as well as other teaching material.

Why go outside the Bible for information? To make a rational decision you must have all the facts. James Sire reminds us that the Bible is not anti-intellectual. "As Christians we know that all truth is God's truth and therefore there is nothing to fear from learning anything which is true. The major problem is error masquerading as truth. But unless we expose ourselves to other points of view and learn to analyze arguments, we may never learn to recognize error."[1]

It's through research that we learn what our choices are

and what we need to know to make an intelligent choice. We need medical information to know whether or not to pull the plug on a terminally ill person. How do physicians determine when an individual is "alive"? Is there a difference of opinion? To decide whether to support or oppose school-based clinics, you need information about their operating procedure. Exactly what kind of sexual counseling takes place?

INFERTILITY

Debbie had to decide about infertility treatment. Three times she and her husband had tried to adopt. The first time the biological mother changed her mind. The second time, when the couple was offered a black child, Debbie's mother-in-law stated firmly that if they went ahead, they should never darken her door again. The third time they contemplated adopting a Romanian child but found out it would cost more than they had.

"My mother-in-law's not a Christian. We had to take that into account. She's a widow. Would we have to cut off contact with her?" They decided not to take the child.

Debbie read all the material on infertility she could get her hands on. "We can't decide about a procedure unless we know enough about it," she said. She and her husband decided to go ahead and she was in treatment for infertility for five years before she became pregnant with her son. For her, the process had included both drugs and intrauterine insemination.

"What I wanted was for God to say plainly that in vitro treatment was permissible under these three criteria." What she had to do instead was to look hard for biblical principles, which she did. "One of the most important was the sanctity of life. I had to be cautious about not hurting others—

even if it was only an embryo. I was to protect and not harm.

"After I had the insemination, I realized that I should have talked with someone who'd been through it beforehand because I hadn't realized that I was responsible for any mix-up or damage to eggs and sperm. They have the potential for life.

"One couple we know had a single infertility test and then decided not to have treatments but accept childlessness as God's will. They'd devote their lives to ministry.

"I asked myself if they were more spiritual than I. But I believe that infertility is a bodily misfunction due to original sin and God has given us scientific advances for treatment. When I became pregnant with my child, the woman said it made her wish she and her husband had had treatment. So she probably hadn't been settled about it in her mind."

In recent years Debbie started a peer support group for women going through infertility. "When women said they were thinking of donor insemination, I was shocked because it didn't seem to fit the unity of marriage. Then I realized there was no biblical mandate against it."

CHECK MANY RESOURCES

To find the most pertinent information without wandering through a literary maze, have your questions clearly formed. Ask your reference librarian and/or bookstore manager to suggest resources. Assess an author's credentials. When reading, look for his or her worldview. Does he argue from a basis of biblical absolutes or relativistic morality?

Ask yourself: Is the author propagandizing? Are his preconceptions accurate? Is he using sound logic when he reasons? Is he drawing conclusions that aren't justified? Is he overstating his case?

Consult more than one resource and make your selection well-rounded. You may *want* to select only authors who endorse the ideas of your family and friends. But that won't provide the whole picture, nor will it enable you to stand on your convictions down the road.

Record statements that provide the most insight and reflect on them prayerfully. On the subject of money, some quotes I'd include would be from *The Golden Cow* by John White. "If . . . we are concerned solely with heavenly treasure and cease to worry about collecting material things, matters which previously puzzled us will fall into place. . . . We must not combat materialism by embracing the opposite error of asceticism. There is no virtue in poverty unless in the course of our obedience to God we have to endure poverty because of a greater end." [2]

The second extrabiblical resource to consult is mature Christian friends. Don't talk to everyone. Avoid people who'll merely pound their bias into you. Choose those who'll tell you objectively how they see it and why. Among the individuals to whom I spoke about artificial insemination, some of the replies I'd prayerfully evaluate in forming my personal conviction are these. They represent both sides of the issue.

A seminary professor: "I'd say it depends on a Christian couple's attitude. If it's 'Well, God won't give us a child, so we'll do it another way'—then their act could be considered arrogant. But if they say, 'We haven't been able to have a child in the usual way and God has allowed new technology that may help us. We enter into that in faith and depend on God,' they could come to quite a different conclusion."

He goes on to state his belief that if a couple goes to the sperm bank and has artificial insemination by donor, the child is the nonbiological father's by the intent of his will.

A priest: "The act of intercourse and procreation are intimately tied together, which is why the church objects to intercourse without procreation. Conversely, it also frowns on conception without intercourse."

A pastor friend: "I'm uncomfortable with the idea of fathering a child biologically, but not through intimacy. The Bible doesn't use the word 'know' when a man went in to have sexual relations with a woman because God was embarrassed to say 'intercourse.' 'Know' implies intimacy and sexual celebration and is interwoven with childbearing. I'm hesitant to tear it apart."

Besides conversations with individuals, participation in groups can be helpful. Perhaps you can request a Sunday School class or a women's Bible class on the subject of moral issues. Look for workshops on subjects you're deciding about. As a friend told me, "You've got to see outside the thing before you make a decision." Since the information you glean will be contradictory, use it to stimulate your own thought processes before God and weigh it carefully.

REEVALUATE

Draw conclusions based on the key thoughts you've read or heard. Throughout the process, your conscience might have been a cautioning parental presence like those of early Jewish Christians who were being asked to eat meat sacrificed to idols. Record what your conscience has to say. Is its input in line with what you're coming to see as true or not?

When I began to reevaluate what I thought about recreational issues, my conscience had a lot to say. *If it's doubtful, it's dirty. You shouldn't support an industry that turns out erotica. It's frowned on by some of the most important Christian leaders you know.*

My conscience made me feel uncertain and guilty. At my most unsure, it almost paralyzed me. But as I gained knowledge, talked with people, and reflected before God, I came to see that conscience was only repeating what it had been taught.

Now it was being retaught. "We should review and examine our moral standard again and again in the light of Scripture in order to evaluate and correct it. It may take time for conscience to adjust to some new or revised item in the moral standard."³

Closely allied with conscience are our feelings and desires about the issue, so record what you *want* to do. I *wanted* to be able to go to a wholesome movie without feeling guilty. I *wanted* to be able to read quality secular fiction without feeling like "one of *them*."

It was important to know how I felt because my feelings strongly influenced my choices. So I had to monitor those desires and decide whether or not my personal feelings and desires ran contrary to some biblical principle. If not, and if the leading of the Holy Spirit or other legitimate factors showed me otherwise, I could conclude that I had liberty to do what I wanted in this instance. The same is true for you.

When you're satisfied that you've researched the issue biblically, gained the extrabiblical information you need as well as a broadened perspective, it's time to review and evaluate your findings. Include your own insights, conclusions based on biblical truths, key thoughts you've read or heard that are a major influence, your conscience's promptings that seem trustworthy, and your desires.

Rethink the question you wrote down at the beginning of the process. Does it still express what you need to know? Does it need to be reworded or expanded?

You now have a mental grasp of the issue about which you need to form a conviction. Put aside your notebook or journal or turn off your computer. Pray to make the best choice you can. Give the information in your mind time to incubate.

Sometimes, there will seem to *be* no "best" choice. So you'll have to decide which accomplishes the greatest good in the biblical sense. Philip Yancey speaks to those of us who want handwriting on the wall. "C.S. Lewis hints at God's 'hesitance' to intervene directly: 'He seems to do nothing of Himself which He can possibly delegate to His creatures. He commands us to do slowly and blunderingly what He could do perfectly and in the twinkling of an eye.' "[4]

That's because His priority is not that we hack our way through the twentieth-century ethical jungle until we find the only pathway and follow it carefully, heel-to-toe as though we've discovered the eleventh or twelfth commandment. His priority is that we cultivate our personal moral dimension — an inner sense of rightness and wrongness that becomes a personal body of truth and a value system by which we choose to live. His priority is not that we have a thundering sense of absoluteness in these areas, because they are not absolutes. We'll grow more secure about our convictions. "Discernment is a habit, not a quick fix. It grows, gradually, like fruit, like the 'fruit of the Spirit.' "[5]

What if you must make a moral choice quickly? First, pray. If you're clinging to some unconfessed sin, repent and be forgiven and cleansed. Consult your Bible for principles that apply and ask your pastor or other mature Christian for help in finding them, if necessary. Ask him or her for insights. If the decision involves modern science or technology, talk with an expert on the subject — a physician on a medical issue, for example.

Expect God to guide as you lean on Him. He lives in you. He is ready and willing to superintend your decision-making process. Then make the most prudent choice you can under the circumstances. God will understand.

One of the toughest moral choices I've witnessed was made by my friend Dale. Diagnosed as having muscular dystrophy at age eleven, doggedly and prayerfully he completed his education and became a professor at Western Baptist College in Salem, Oregon. However, in 1983 he resigned due to deteriorating health. Although he could no longer breathe without a respirator, he worked at his computer, journeyed to town in his wheelchair, and played fiercely competitive games of Rook every Friday evening with his friend Ruth and whatever unsuspecting partners they'd lined up.

In 1991, due to the deterioration of his body, Dale could no longer eat or digest food. In the hospital, he had to make a choice: should he go to a nursing home and be kept alive by a machine? Or should he have hospital personnel pull the plug?

We heard that he'd made the choice. He would not go to a nursing home. He would have the medical staff pull the plug in the hospital.

Dale knew Scripture; he'd been studying it systematically all his adult life. The next few days, he talked over his choice with church staff, family, and friends. The hospital ethics committee met and approved his decision.

John and I went to see him in the hospital after he'd made his decision. With each respirator breath, he gasped out reasons why he'd made the choice he had. "I only have the prospect of getting worse . . . pain and suffering. . . . "

Before he left, he recited what he said was his favorite verse from one of his favorite hymns — "Guide Me O Thou Great Jehovah."

When I tread the verge of Jordan,
Bid my anxious fears subside;
Death of death, and hell's destruction,
Land me safe on Canaan's side.

Hospital personnel disconnected the machines. Dale breathed on his own for a time. Then, as he had wished, he went to be with the Lord.

1. James W. Sire, *How to Read Slowly* (Downers Grove, Ill.: InterVarsity Press, 1978), p. 145.
2. John White, *The Golden Cow* (Downers Grove, Ill.: InterVarsity Press, 1979), pp. 47, 57.
3. Milton L. Rudnick, *Christian Ethics for Today* (Grand Rapids: Baker Book House, 1979), p. 77.
4. Philip Yancey, "Decision Making: A Credible Alternative to Confusion," *Moody Monthly*, November 1984, p. 22.
5. Peter Kreeft, *Making Choices* (Ann Arbor: Servant Books, 1990), p. 199.

Living by Our Convictions

NINE ❦

*I*t's urgent that we be sure we *do* have a genuine conviction. A woman might *believe* that abortion is wrong except under extreme circumstances.

But if she became pregnant outside marriage while a college student and the man couldn't or wouldn't support her — her *belief* might not be strong enough to influence her decision.

Another woman might *prefer* not to sell shoddy merchandise for a company whose ethics are questionable but still tell herself that business is business and God knows she can't afford to quit.

A third might be of the *opinion* that voting is important but not take time to become informed about candidates and issues and, as a result, stay away from the polls at election time.

DEFINITION OF CONVICTIONS

As we have seen, convictions are neither beliefs, preferences, nor opinions. They are that to which we hold wholeheartedly and of which we are convinced. *Being responsible to program porn is wrong. Lying for the boss is wrong. So is having an abortion to end an unwanted pregnancy, promotion of shoddy merchandise for an unethical company, and not becoming an informed voter. So I choose to act on what I am convinced is moral.*

But there will be a cost—small or great—from taking time to investigate candidates' qualifications and issues, to going through a pregnancy alone. Jesus warned us to take that cost into account.

"Suppose one of you wants to build a tower. Will he not first sit down and estimate the cost to see if he has enough money to complete it? . . . Or suppose a king is about to go to war against another king. Will he not first sit down and consider whether he is able with ten thousand men to oppose the one coming against him with twenty thousand?" (Luke 14:28, 31)

So we'll be able to stand despite the push and shove from all sides to do otherwise, Jesus advises us to ask ourselves two things:

1. What might this conviction cost me?
2. On what resources can I count?

Some of the things living by a conviction has cost people I talked with are these:

Inconvenience. "We decided not to spend money on Sunday and not to engage in any activity whenever possible that requires others to work that day."

Loss of family support. "My family thought I was going overboard for religion. Because I wouldn't participate in certain activities, there was a barrier between us for a long time and I felt very much alone."

Career and financial loss. "I had an opportunity to teach at a Christian school or a public school. I opted for a Christian school even though the pay is less and there's no retirement plan."

Unfulfilled desire. "Several years after I became a widow, a man propositioned me, 'We're alone and could find great enjoyment together.' Part of me thought the idea didn't sound too bad. But I knew it was wrong."

Loss of friends. "When a friend did something wrong, I stayed by her. Others thought I should separate myself from her. I even seemed to suffer some kind of guilt by association."

Loss of social status. "There are times when I have to say no to old friends' invitations and stay home alone. It gets lonely and I'm tempted sometimes to go along anyway."

To choose to act on a conviction when a job or a friendship or a lifestyle is at stake requires the same leap of faith that my friend Michelle took when she jumped out of a plane and pulled the ripcord for the first time.

OUR SOURCES OF STRENGTH

On whom can we depend when we're called to take a risk for the sake of our values?

God the Father. "The Lord is my strength" (Ex. 15:2).

Jesus Christ the Son. "I will be with you always" (Matt. 28:20).

God the Holy Spirit. "You will receive power when the Holy Spirit comes on you; and you will be My witnesses" (Acts 1:8).

To make the leap of faith requires an act of our will. Although I was afraid to make choices different from those close to me for fear of alienating them, finally I understood that doing so is part of my God-given responsibility. Gradually, the apostles' words that "we must obey God rather than men," seemed to become timber in my soul (Acts 5:29).

Helen remembers when she had to choose and act. "I loved to watch a particular soap opera. As my daughter got older, she'd sit and watch it with me. I had to stop and ask myself: 'Do I want her taking in this stuff? Do I want it stored in her mind?' "

Helen decided that not only was it unhealthy for her daughter, but it was unhealthy for her. She decided to sever their ties with soaps and to explain why.

We do have to *learn* to live by a particular conviction. It must be tested, like a new pair of jeans whose durability is potential but not proven until the owner wears them while climbing and crawling and shinnying.

About a dozen years ago, I was torn as to whether or not I should stop writing for publication and get a secular job. Money was scarce but ministry was my love. After working through the process, I became convinced that I should continue writing, even though it was not as financially lucrative.

That's when the test began. Was my conviction strong enough to carry me through the lean times? I didn't know. Often, I fought fear. But deeper than my fear was a growing sense of assurance from God that I had concluded correctly and that I was called to live by faith.

It's the test of a conviction that proves its genuineness. I was discussing this point over lunch with several women during a weekend retreat at which I was speaking. Cherry's face lit up.

"Once, I bit into one of the oysters my husband and I had picked up on the beach and I felt something crunch. What I spit out looked like a tiny pearl!

"We took it to a jeweler and he said he could test it. 'If it's genuine, it will withstand the test. If not, it'll dissolve.' He asked if we wanted to take the chance.

"We said we did. It survived. We had a real pearl."

When it passes the test, our conviction becomes part of us. *Yes. This is what I believe. This is what I want to live by.*

If we discover flaws, it's time to stop and think through the process again. Do we need a stronger biblical foundation? More factual information? Time to reflect and pray?

CIRCUMSTANCES

The way in which a conviction influences our behavior depends on circumstances. Not every moral choice carries with it a mandate to carry a placard or take a frightening risk. Right now the only way you're required to act on your view of cosmetic surgery may be by saying what you personally think in a conversation with your neighbor when the subject arises. Years from now, when your chin sags, frown lines have become permanent furrows, and TV talk shows promote surgical youth, you'll be called to go from talk to action. *Will I keep the face I've got or buy a younger one?*

If it's a decision not to watch squirming and moaning beneath the sheets on TV when you're alone, you'll probably begin by switching the dial when a scene begins. Next, you'll feel called on to tell others with whom you do your viewing how you feel. Later, you may sense an obligation to act further on your decision by writing a network and complaining about erotica on prime time. If that gets little results, you may start boycotting advertisers of sexy programs.

For Tina, living by her conviction about Halloween has taken planning. "My parents let me go trick-or-treating, but I don't let my kids go. I explain to them what the Bible says about evil spirits and that we should stay away from things like that.

"Instead, I either take them to a church party or have one myself. If I give the party, we don't have black cats for decorations, but we do have a pumpkin hunt (which is hunting for candy). We make jack-o'-lanterns and talk about the fact that God likes bright colors, gives us good food to eat, and seeds so we'll continue to have food. The candle shining through the jack-o'-lantern illustrates the fact that God wants us to let His light shine through us in the world."

Now that we *do have* a conviction about the homeless or sex as a single, should we expect to *always* stand uncompromisingly like the heroine in a turn-of-the-century novel? Blond hair blowing in the wind, skirts flapping around her ankles, chin firm, eyes brimming with tears, she watches as her beloved leaves her for the last time. He smiles sardonically at her because she simply will not compromise.

We should *aim* to stand—steadfast, unmovable—but without thinking more highly of ourselves than we ought to think. For we are *not* cardboard characters manipulated by pen and plotline. We are fallible human beings with passions and drives who are still under the influence of our sin nature.

Does that mean that *we* are failures? Hardly. We are *learners* who, by the grace of God, Christ's nature in us, and the Holy Spirit, are toddling in His steps.

"Failure should be our teacher, not our undertaker. Failure is delay, not defeat. It is a temporary detour, not a dead-end street."[1]

How can failure become our teacher?

1. Decide why you failed. If you were Peter, what reason would you pinpoint as to why you denied knowing Jesus just before His crucifixion? If you were honest, you couldn't escape the fact that you were just plain scared that you'd be arrested and killed too. No blaming someone else; no excuses. *I was scared.*

If you were David, why would you say that you committed

adultery with Bathsheba and had her husband killed even though it was absolutely anathema to your moral value system? *Lust. I wanted Bathsheba so badly that I allowed nothing or no one to stand in the way.*

2. Evaluate your commitment. *Have I honestly counted the cost?* "If anyone would come after Me, he must deny himself and take up his cross and follow Me" (Matt. 16:24).

"I don't love my husband anymore," one woman told me. "But I believe divorce is only for extreme situations, and I have to give God a chance to bond Bill and me. So I'm letting go daily of my desire to have a fulfilling marital relationship now and am trusting God to answer prayer and show us how to bring love back into our marriage."

Living by our convictions has a price tag that calls for deep pockets. So does humbling ourselves and asking for help to break a habit that keeps us short of our goal. Jesus makes it plain: to have the courage of our convictions means we must deny the piece of self that stubbornly digs in against His will.

Some failures may be because someone close to us—our husband perhaps—so strongly disagrees with our stand that our relationship is threatened. In the next chapter, we'll look at steps to take when that happens.

If your courage fails the way Peter's did, tell God your sorrow. Receive forgiveness and cleansing. Count on the fact that God is your *Father* and you are His *girl child.* Like a loving Father whose little girl has fallen, He'll wipe you clean and hold your hand as you get up and toddle onward.

Through His Word, He'll encourage you to keep going. "His incomparably great power for us . . . is like the working of His mighty strength which He exerted in Christ when He raised Him from the dead" (Eph. 1:19-20).

Through the members of His body, He'll provide steadying arms. Seek them out. Count on the spiritual strength the Father will provide once you choose to act on what He shows you. Count on the presence of the living Son of God. Count on the Holy Spirit—your Comforter, Teacher, and Guide.

NEVER LOOK BACK

Darcie and Bob Jones had to do that when they faced probably the toughest decision of their lives. "Whatever decision we made, Bob and I had to make it together and never look back," she says.

After two years of infertility treatment, Darcie was pregnant. During ultrasound at nine weeks, an expressionless technician counted aloud what he saw on the screen: "There's one baby, there's two, there's three, there's four, there's . . . there's four babies."

His next words shocked Darcie. "I'm sorry." Stunned and overwhelmed at the news, she was even more confused when her infertility specialist's nurse, whom Darcie knew well, burst into tears when told about the quadruplets.

The doctor's "Congratulations" was the first positive word she heard. "He went on to explain that we had three options and explained the risks of each. First, we could continue the pregnancy as it was. That would be very hard on me; for one thing, I could develop toxemia.

"Our second choice was selective elimination. If Bob and I chose that, the doctor would abort one or more of the babies by injecting saline solution into a baby's heart. That way, the remaining children would have a better chance of survival." He also let the Joneses know that in the process a remaining baby could be damaged.

"The third choice was to abort the pregnancy and start over."

Bob and Darcie had two weeks to decide. "Before we were confronted with this choice, I'd gone along with the crowd on the subject of abortion. It's one thing to march in a rally; it's another to come face-to-face with it in your own life.

"We wanted to make a wise, educated, prayerful decision so we had to consider all the options. People are appalled at that. But to do anything less is to make an ignorant decision.

"One evening we went away and spent the hours crying and praying and hugging. Finally I looked at Bob. 'God has been so faithful to give us this gift; He's not going to bail out on us now.' To question whether or not He'd continue to be faithful seemed ludicrous." They would not abort any of the babies; instead, they'd entrust them to Him and count on His perfect will. The life or death of their babies belonged in His hands, not theirs.

"Once we made our decision, I didn't question it. There were times when I was scared that something would be wrong with the babies. So many things could go wrong, I had to consciously fix my eyes on hope." Darcie was hospitalized for the last six weeks and suffered from toxemia the last two of those weeks.

A couple who were the parents of quads sent Darcie a photo of their four children. "I took it with me to the hospital and posted it next to my bed. They were the embodiment of God's promise that it could be OK."

The doctor wanted Darcie to carry the babies for seven months if she possibly could; they were delivered on July 14, 1991 at thirty-two weeks. On Palm Sunday 1992, Bob and Darcie Jones stood on the church platform with their own four healthy babies to be dedicated—two boys and two girls.

At the end of the family group was Ian, the smallest of the four. If the Joneses had chosen selective elimination, he was the child who wouldn't have been there that morning.

1. William A. Ward, compiled by Lloyd Cory, *Quotable Quotations* (Wheaton, Ill.: Victor Books, 1985), p. 127.

The Kathleen Swan Story

In October 1985, a new worker in the daycare where Bill and Kathleen Swan (their real names) had left their three-year-old daughter told the little girl that "nobody must see your private parts." To this the child answered, "Mommy and Daddy do." The worker then questioned the girl further about possible sexual abuse.

This same worker believes that most people abuse their children and that she herself was abused almost daily by up to 400 different people in her early years. Previously she had reported 22 cases of abuse.

A Shelter Care Hearing followed and the child was removed from the Swan home. The couple was presented with a list of therapists who specialize in diagnosing and treating sexual deviancy. "We were told to go and be tested and 'get into treatment'—and *then* they would see about visits with our daughter," says Kathy Swan. "I felt violated, insulted, almost as though I were being asked to submit to a rape in order to prove I wasn't a danger to my own child."

The Swans would be required to admit guilt, "otherwise we were in denial and therefore untreatable and remained a threat to the community's safety.

"How could I do that?" Kathy asks. "I have *never* abused my child. She means the world to me. My life was Christ's but my daughter occupied a very important place in my heart.

"Would I have to *lie* in order to accomplish my heart's much-needed relief? As a child of God, I am required to live uprightly and speak the truth, no matter what the consequences may be. Cost is irrelevant.

"Second, the test involves delving into pornography and twisted relationships and I am prohibited from engaging in and considering such filth by virtue of who lives in me. The temptation to do what was expedient for me was tremendously strong and real.

"The bottom line for me was: 'Whom do I trust—man or God?' But what if the price is too high?

"In prayer and seeking counsel from trusted sisters and brothers and in consulting the Word of God, I found ample support for the belief that I could withstand the trial and come out victoriously. Our attorney also advised us not to pursue the tests and so we refused."

Kathy firmly believed that "God gives people gifts in order to enable them to make correct choices for their well-being. One is a mind to ponder His truth and to reason out any decision to its conclusion. He also gives human counselors, His still small voice within, and wisdom if we ask (James 1:5). It seems appropriate to take all available information into account, carefully weigh the cost and consequences, and then move out in faith.

"The refusal set in motion the machinery that would eventually charge and convict us of a heinous crime—statutory rape in the first degree: two counts."

Before trial in April 1986, the prosecutor offered the couple a deal: plead guilty to first-degree incest upon their daughter; in exchange the prosecution would drop additional charges that involved Kathy's best friend's child.

If Bill and Kathy went along, their sentence would be only nine months in jail, a year's probation, and treatment with a view toward visitation with their daughter.

"The offer was quite tempting, especially when I learned that if she prevailed, the prosecutor was going to ask for an exceptional sentence of double the high end of the allowable range—one hundred months!

"Wouldn't Jesus understand it was too much to ask me to serve eight years for a crime I did not commit? I was reminded that Joseph was accused and convicted on false testimony too. Though he spent years in prison, he was ultimately vindicated and became the vehicle for the rescue of all of Israel from starvation.

"Then there is the Lord Jesus Christ who willingly bore the insults of an unjust conviction and execution only to be raised from the dead in victory and power.

"The message to me seemed clear: either I acted in accord with my beliefs or I had no integrity.

"What about the price? I did consider it, but compared with the act of moral and spiritual suicide I was being asked to commit, it was small."

Kathy and Bill Swan were convicted and each sentenced to four years in prison. The evidence of their innocence was so powerful that "Sixty Minutes" aired their story in March 1992. That program pointed out that no physical examination of the child was done until five years after the alleged crime. When such an examination finally did take place, it was discovered that the child's hymen was still intact despite the allegation that rape supposedly occurred. A hymen does not grow back.

What does a woman do when faced with such a wrenching dilemma? Kathy's answer: "Take all the available information into account, carefully weigh the cost and consequences, and then move out in faith. We will all stand before the Lord one day and give account for how we used the gifts He gave us to live holy lives and produce fruit for Him in our lives."

When Convictions Conflict

TEN ❦

*I*t doesn't take long to figure out that if we're going to stand for what we honestly believe, conflicts are inevitable. It was because of heated exchanges over such differences described in Acts 15 that the apostles met for the first Jerusalem Council.

The dispute was fiery then and it can get fiery for us today. The minute we view others as suspect because, for example, they disagree with our stand that the government should give priority to the subsidization of daycare for needy moms, "one-in-the-Spirit" is very likely to begin to deteriorate.

That two-camp dichotomy is illustrated in the company that published this book. For, although all departments are housed in one building, part of that building resides in the city of Wheaton and part in the city of Glen Ellyn.

One woman described how she and her husband planted

their feet on different turf and stood firm. "I believed my children should *not* apply for federal aid for college funds and my husband thought they should. Feelings were fierce. He finally dropped the subject. Later, I wondered if I was wrong."

FAMILY RELATIONSHIPS

Family relationships are one important area where the fire flares, and women tell me that television and videos are a major source of differences. "My husband can tolerate more violent and risqué scenes than I can," I heard often. "If I object, he is upset with me. I try leaving the room, but that doesn't work either. What bothers me most is that he allows our kids to watch things I think they shouldn't."

A Bible college professor said, "As a faculty, we've gone round and round on the wine issue. None of us approves of drunkenness. But there are some members who believe Christians should never use alcohol. Others believe that wine is a gift of God."

Some singles don't let their parents know some of the things they do for entertainment because of the inevitable explosion. "Recently, I told them I was going to a Paul Simon concert and they were appalled. I don't know why I mentioned it at all."

Other areas of major disagreements include . . .

Business Ethics. "I showed a client every available house in his price range," Nancy, a realtor friend, told me. "He didn't like any of them. The following Sunday I saw an ad in the newspaper for a house that sounded just like what the client wanted. But the owner wouldn't let me show it.

"If the client had asked me about the house, I would have told him he'd have to see it on his own." But when my realtor friend told someone about the situation, she was told that she acted wrongly. "You should have called the client and told him about the house." But Nancy didn't believe that was her responsibility.

A teacher described the professional differences she faces. "If I passed a child but stipulated that he or she had to accomplish certain things to enter the next level, the principal was likely to reverse my stipulation because of pressure from the parents."

Sexual Practices. "My husband wants me to participate in acts that I feel are perverted and wrong. When I told him how I felt, he accused me of being narrow-minded. Our differences have seriously affected our sex life . . . and our general closeness as well."

Social Issues. One longtime friend left the church when members strongly objected to his participation in an antinuclear demonstration. Especially sensitive to human suffering because he'd traveled around the world and walked among outcasts in places like the streets of Calcutta, he couldn't understand their endorsement of what he considered to be the potential source of the worst human suffering. They couldn't understand what they saw as his radical stance.

Besides these, there are a Heinz 57 variety of other issues that generate controversy.

Christian College Students. Student dress codes and after-class social rules to which kids object.

Procreation. "We recently became convinced not to use birth control." Not a popular stand, even among Christians.

Even Death. "I can't see how a Christian could endorse cremation. But some I know do."

Because we Christians are used to dealing in absolutes, part of our minds keeps stubbornly insisting that there must be absolutes about everything.

The main character in Joseph Bayly's story, "A Small Happening at Andover" echoes that mind-set. "She told the Lord that He knew — *He knew* that there was only one right way for a thing to be. . . . Accordingly, she asked Him to show her which was right: whether the African violet she had purchased at Dustin's Greenhouse that afternoon should be placed on the right or left end of the bookcase."[1]

DIVERSITY AND COMPLEXITY

Few of us expect that degree of rightness. Still, life would be so much more simple if that were the case. Diversity within the body of Christ creates complexity and, to some, it smacks of relativism.

The fact is, there are legitimate reasons why we differ.

Old Covenant, New Covenant. "My brother believes we should be under Old Testament dietary laws and I do not. It creates a hassle during family gatherings when we all sit down to a meal Mom has cooked."

What's the Principle? A biblical teaching may be interpreted very differently by individuals. Take "avoid sexual immorality" (1 Thes. 4:3). To one it may indicate pristine purity. To another it could allow certain behaviors because she doesn't classify them as immoral.

A kind, generous Christian woman I knew believed strongly that blacks are inferior, and she used verses from Scripture to substantiate her stand. I just as strongly believed that she had grossly misinterpreted them and had been influenced by off-track extrabiblical writings.

Where You've Been. Elisabeth Elliot, former missionary to Auca Indians, says, "In America a man who switched a naked child with nettles would be called a sadist. Aucas consider this a legitimate and effective form of punishment and were outraged to see me spank my three-year-old child. I was to them, a savage."[2]

The same differences exist close to home. "The church we were attending taught strict discipline of our toddlers. Friends outside that church strongly disagreed."

A middle-aged woman remembered her early years. "I was raised in a very strict church and my husband was not. I was strongly influenced by what I'd been taught and that bothered him sometimes."

Who You Are. Conservative. Cautious. Or radically minded and a risk taker.

Although we have been given a godly nature and are indwelt by the Holy Spirit, we are still individuals and some of our ethical views reflect our human identity.

How can we disagree and still get along with husband, parents, siblings, coworkers, church members, and friends? With a roommate who is sold on a computer dating service and keeps insisting we should register too even though we don't believe it's God's way for us to find the mate of our dreams? With a partner whose idea of adequate housing for migrant workers doesn't even begin to measure up to ours?

Keep in mind at the outset of the confrontation that everyone who opposes us may not have a well-thought-out, biblically founded conviction by which they have chosen to live. Margo's husband wanted her to vacation with him in Las Vegas. "I have personal convictions against gambling," Margo told me. "Dick is moral, and he simply sees no reason why he shouldn't do this because it's enjoyment—so long as he uses restraint."

When it comes to handling these conflicts, we cannot play the role of the kangaroo and the emu who stand face-to-face in the Australian coat of arms.

Neither of these animals can back up—the kangaroo because of its tail and the emu because of its three great toes on the front of its feet.

TALK TO EACH OTHER

As if that's not bad enough, neither can they talk things out. But we human beings can—and must. To do that . . .

1. *Handle emotions first.* When one couple's son was born mentally retarded and the attending physician recommended they institutionalize him, the couple felt as though their insides had turned to sawdust.

Should they go along? Too devastated at first to think clearly, they fired feeling-couched statements at one another.

"I don't see how you can expect me to take him home. I just can't handle it."

"And I don't see how you can send him away. He's our *son.*"

It was only when they talked with a counselor that they saw the necessity to let their feelings settle before they made a *final* decision.

It does make sense to agree to cool off when tempers first begin to flare. Then, after each asks for personal insight from God, the two can address the issue. By then, probably, at least some of the unimportant factors will fall into perspective.

"The listener may argue with your opinions and consider his own opinions just as good. He will resist your moralizing, blaming, judging, and condeming. But when you say how you feel without attacking him for creating those feelings, you are most likely to be heard."[3]

2. *Review your conviction.* During a conversation with someone on the subject of morality, the other person stopped mid-sentence when talking about a particular issue. "Do I have a conviction or only a preference? I'm not sure." We may not be sure either. I did not have a *conviction* about my nursing home ministry, I realized when confronted with another opinion. But the principle of showing love to my neighbor and aiding the needy were biblical grounds.

3. *Talk it over.* Keep remembering that it isn't possible to reason with emotions. Remember too that your purpose isn't to persuade the other person that you're right. It's to gain an understanding of the other's position.

So hear the other person out and request she do the same for you. Ask questions to help her tell you why she thinks as she does. Try to talk facts. Find out what foundation she has for her belief.

4. *Assess your attitudes.* "Do I secretly want only to convince the other that I'm right? Am I overreacting because I feel attacked? Are old resentments playing a role?"

"Because my folks were so strict I couldn't even sew doll clothes on Sunday I have to let go of yesterday when Mom and I confront a moral difference today."

Conflicts between husband and wife are the ones that seem to rub most women raw. I had unrealistic expectations, perhaps stemming from the romantic notion that lovers always see alike. That's one reason it upset me terribly when I began to formulate convictions and John and I didn't agree. To think differently threatened my feeling of acceptance by him. To have him defend his views impassionedly scared me.

Over and over he'd say, "We don't have to think alike on every issue for me to love you. One has nothing to do with the other."

Because I was insecure it took me years to grasp that principle. Until I grew up as a person, I'd often dissolve in tears during disagreements, half hoping John would acquiesce to placate me.

A RIGHT TO CONVICTIONS

As I've said, I know now that I have a right — even an obligation — to my own convictions and a right to express them.

Placating me would have been the worst thing John could have done. Becoming certain of my role as a Christian woman and wife had been vital.

Every Christian woman needs to keep before her the biblical description of who she is. Because society's idea of a woman is so splintered, we need to keep God's view central. Ron and Beverly Allen in their book, *Liberated Traditionalism,* summarized His view better than any authors I've read.

● Since God created man as male and female, both bear His image (Gen. 1:27).

● Both sexes are commissioned to rule the earth (v. 28).

● Woman was taken from man, so she is of the same essence as he (2:21).

● She has a name comparable to his, citing her as equal (v. 23).

● Man and woman become one flesh so they're equal as persons (v. 24).

The New Testament states it plainly. "There is neither Jew nor Greek, slave nor free, male nor female, for you are all one in Christ Jesus" (Gal. 3:28).

Besides this, a correct understanding of two words is a key to accepting our rights as women to form our own convictions. The first is *headship.* "Because the man was created prior to the woman . . . he exercises a level of headship over her . . . the woman is equal to the man, but the man is the head of the woman."[4]

The "head" is someone in a position of leadership. The concept is based on Christ's headship of the church. Not only is Christ the Leader, but He also helps us who are members of His body to grow.

The second is *submission.* Paul's words "Wives, submit to your husbands as to the Lord" (Eph. 5:22), is not a door slammed in our faces — because it directly follows the apostle's words, "Submit to one another out of reverence for

Christ" (v. 21). As the rest of the chapter shows and the tone of the New Testament emphasizes, it's mutual forbearance in love that is the way of the Christian life.

So in matters to do with our marriage, after discussion in which we seriously hear and reflect on the other's views, our husband makes the final decision. In her business relationships and in areas that have to do with her personal morality, the husband and wife may talk about an issue but the wife will make the final decision.

Because husband and wife are equals, when convictions conflict we play by the same rules as in any other relationship. "Be completely humble and gentle; be patient, bearing with one another in love" (4:2).

There are times when we're called to do the unthinkable — and compromise — a word that reeks with negative connotation so far as morality is concerned. But it simply means "to make concessions." So we're not talking about wimping out and rejecting the faith, but acquiescing in nonessentials.

When deciding if compromise is in order, ask yourself: "Is this an issue on which the Bible gives a command? Or can its teachings and principles be interpreted differently?" Perhaps you've believed so strongly that you haven't been able to imagine someone holding a different, biblically founded view, but now you've come to see that it's possible.

Discuss and Negotiate. Some members of your family are pretty capable of using the TV set judiciously, but even they occasionally do watch shows that are degrading. Others in the family seem to have little self-control so far as television viewing is concerned. At family meetings, you talk about what to do and decide to try living without a set for three months and renegotiate when the test period is over.

Choose the Greater Good. Because ours is a fallen society, there are often no perfect solutions. Choose the greater good was what Debbie had to do when she and her husband were confronted with . . .

. . . either adopting a black child and alienating her non-Christian, widowed mother-in-law

. . . or refusing the child to protect her relationship with the woman.

Neither choice was completely satisfying, but the couple did what seemed to them to be best.

Peaceful Coexistence. Christians are not photocopies of one another. What your conscience allows, mine may not. I may have lived a more protected life than you. You may have reached a level of spiritual maturity to which I haven't attained yet.

Instead of bringing out your ammunition, we can agree to disagree. You're convinced it's OK for you, as the mother of small children, to work outside your home and your sister does not? Be a good listener, agree with any of her statements you can, be sure she knows you respect her as a person, and let her know you expect the same from her. Don't expect her to baby-sit your children when you're at work, of course.

Let's face it, peaceful coexistence isn't always possible. "When I try to tell my husband quietly that the R-rated videos he brings home are too much for me, he gets mad. What am I supposed to do?"

Get help. Very likely, your problem isn't a disagreement over videos. It goes deeper than that. You both need to talk with a mature, informed, neutral third party about things like old resentments, unresolved issues, and better ways to communicate.

The same holds true for a standoff with your roommate, a church member, or extended family member. As soon as they agree to do so, sit down with an intermediary. That's vital because, although you may have stopped *talking* about the disagreement, neither of you has stopped *thinking* about it. Instead of warmth between you, a big chill may set in.

TAKING A STAND

When convictions conflict, you may have to *take a stand*. When he says, "This way" and you say, "That way," you try to negotiate and work out a compromise. Or you agree to disagree and peacefully coexist.

If, on these teeth-gritting occasions, neither action works and you have to take a stand, "Make every effort to keep the unity of the Spirit through the bond of peace . . . until we all reach unity in the faith and in the knowledge of the Son of God and become mature, attaining to the whole measure of the fullness of Christ" (Eph. 4:3, 13).

"Make every effort." Don't settle either for peace at any price or living in a cold war because your efforts at mutual understanding were rebuffed once.

"Keep the unity of the Spirit." Work (and it *is* work) to maintain not *uniformity* of views, but *unity*—deep spiritual ties because we share the nature of Christ. Because we are called to be one just as the Father and Son are One. Because we are each indwelled with the Holy Spirit of God who is love, peace, patience, kindness, gentleness, and self-control in us. It's our loving acceptance of one another *despite* our differences that's the miracle.

"Until . . . the [daughters] of God . . . become mature, attaining to the whole measure of the fullness of Christ" (bracketed word mine).

That's tomorrow—in eternity.

For today, in the here and now . . .

maintain the eternal perspective.

1. Joseph Bayly, *How Silently, How Silently* (Elgin, Ill.: David C. Cook Publishing Co., 1968), p. 35.
2. Elisabeth Elliot, *The Liberty of Obedience* (Waco, Texas: Word Books, 1968), p. 16.
3. Andre Bustanoby, *Just Talk to Me* (Grand Rapids: Zondervan Publishing Co., 1981), p. 85.

4. Ronald and Beverly Allen, *Liberated Traditionalism* (Portland, Ore.: Multnomah, 1985), p. 124.

To Change or Not to Change?

ELEVEN 🍒

As little girls, we crave the security of the familiar. The same teddy bear, the same bedtime routine. That craving doesn't disappear simply because we've become big ladies.

There are also times when the sameness of life turns our days gray and our insides scream for a break from the familiar. *What I need is a weekend getaway instead of the same old Saturday housecleaning and grocery shopping routine.* Mostly though, we are apt to cling to the familiar for security and feel vaguely uneasy when it's taken from us.

CHANGE IS PART OF LIFE

So it's no wonder that most of us eye change in one of the most important areas of all—our moral value system—with profound suspicion. The idea smacks of spiritual deterioration. But change is as much a part of human life as is growing up and growing old.

We *do* change our convictions — sometimes with good reason. Peter did. His story begins one noontime after Pentecost when that apostle climbed to his upstairs porch to pray.

He had a vision. The heavens opened and Peter saw something like a large sheet filled with clean and unclean animals being let down to earth, and heard a voice commanding him to "Get up, Peter. Kill and eat" (Acts 10:13).

The big, bombastic fisherman, who'd lived for three years with the Messiah, who'd stumbled through the confusion of the Crucifixion and the shock of the Resurrection and probably thought he'd seen it all, was incredulous. A paradigm of religious virtue, like all scrupulous Jews he was particular about what he ate. No one would convince him to stop for a pork chop dinner.

So of course he politely declined God's invitation. God repeated the scenario two more times. When the vision was over, Peter still wasn't sure what it meant. He finally understood only when God explained through an experience — a visit to the Roman centurion, Cornelius.

The Lord Almighty had prepared Cornelius to hear the Gospel about Jesus Christ and Peter to deliver it. In a very short time, Peter's convictions had done a complete turnabout! Instead of exclusion based on the Law, he was ready to live by the inclusion of grace.

"You are well aware that it is against our law for a Jew to associate with a Gentile or visit him. But God has shown me that I should not call any man impure or unclean" (v. 28).

Peter's radical change of moral view was the result of a direct *revelation* from God — necessary because the New Testament was not yet written. Today though, that Book is in our hands or on our nightstands. When we change our moral view because of doctrine, instead of *revelation* of a heretofore unknown truth, it's because of *insight* into truth already revealed.

INSIGHT

Insight is the ability to see and understand in a way we didn't before. It happens for a variety of reasons.

● We've grown more confident as women so we've developed confidence that God will give us a broader, deeper view of His Word. Lately, we realize, that's just what He's been doing. "I keep asking that the God of our Lord Jesus Christ, the glorious Father, may give you the Spirit of wisdom and revelation, so that you may know Him better. I pray also that the eyes of your heart may be enlightened" (Eph. 1:17-18). *That means me.*

● We've become better Bible students than we were, so we have better ability to formulate biblical principles. Although she was a longtime Christian and active in church, it wasn't until about a year ago that a woman friend in her thirties began to learn how to exegete Scripture correctly and deduce its central truths. As a result of the fact that she's more facile with the Word of God, she enjoys digging more deeply than before.

● We have more time and/or inclination to be reflective. Before, life seemed to be a long series of meetings and appointments and eating and sleeping. Or we were hard at keeping our kids and the neighbors' from turning one more brief skirmish into a major melee. Now, things have slowed down. Perhaps we have taken charge of our lives in the Lord and have made time to think about biblical principles.

● We've gained more experience in prayer and in hearing the inner silent voice of the Holy Spirit of God as He illuminates the Bible that He inspired.

The reasons I began changing my moral views were—all of the above. Yes, I was more confident that I could see for myself. Since my conversion I'd studied the Bible, but in recent years I'd become more skillful at it—mostly because I'd ingested the principles of scholars like R.C. Sproul, Gordon Fee, Douglas Stuart, Irving Jensen, and Kenneth Wuest.

I wasn't thinking more about the biblical foundations for moral issues now only because I had more time. Sons John, Paul, and Mark *were grown* and gone from home—but my professional commitments had increased enormously. Rather, I'd been growing much more quiet inside. That's because I'd been cultivating the habit of resting in the Lord. Becoming quiet inside provided the right environment in which to think issues through. Then too as the silence grew, so did my ability to sense God's illumination.

Another reason for change may be that we may also find our perception of what's right in a particular moral issue is evolving because *we're* evolving—from legalistic perfectionism to freedom. That may be happening because we're being healed from emotional damage. I meet scores of women like that. Like me, they've been desperate to please. Women like us spent our early years in Christ walking heel to toe across a religious high wire, scrupulously trying to "do it right," as though the ringmaster stood below wielding a whip.

Finally, because the Holy Spirit is faithful, we began to see: we are not high-wire performers. We are adopted daughters. God is no whip-wielding Ringmaster. He is Father and home.

● I went through a period in my Christian life when I was very rigid in my moral views. If I did any work on a Sunday, for example, I felt terribly guilty. Use of wine—even in cooking—scared me. All my moral choices were made with the idea that God was ready to jump on me for the smallest infractions.

● The more I absorbed the love of God and the fact that Christ kept the law for me because I could not, the more I was able to get out from under the burden of the law. Of course, I still lived by absolutes when the Bible stated them, but now in the rest of life, I was free to live by the leading of the Holy Spirit as He illuminated and applied scriptural principles.

● Two of Paul's teachings became very important to me. "Live by the Spirit," and "Serve one another in love" (Gal. 5:16, 13).

CHANGING

On the other hand, self-assured feminist Christians often change because they come to see that the ideas they held so strongly were not necessarily all God's ideas. About abortion, perhaps. Or stay-at-home wives or mothers. Or what's moral and what's not in order to get ahead in one's career.

We may change simply because we're separating from others and becoming our own person. Women told me that it was when they were exposed to a broader spectrum of people and ideas that their convictions began to change. What was really happening for some, though, was that they were moving forward from mere beliefs or preferences to personal convictions. Old ideas had not been based on their best understanding of biblical principles but on views of family or peers or church. So they reexamine, reevaluate, and sometimes reshape.

A minister's wife said that she and her husband tried for a long time to choose moral behavior for themselves and their children that would please their congregations. "Finally we had to face the fact that this simply wasn't working. Some people were against going to the movies but celebrated Halloween by trick-or-treating, etc. Others thought going to movies was OK but celebrating Halloween was not. All we were doing was raising people-pleasers." They began to form convictions as a family and live by these instead.

New experiences can also nudge us to switch from one side of the fence to the other. Suppose . . .

● Someone close to you is sent to prison. Now, instead of secondhand information about conditions behind bars, you learn about them firsthand. Before, you sounded off about turning prisons into resorts. Now, while you know that may be true in some situations, you also know that reform is an absolute must. You say when the subject comes up, that we have got to work for rehabilitation — especially through prison ministries.

● You sign up to go to the inner-city slums on a two-week mission. Shocked by garbage-littered streets and rat-infested cold water flats, the words "ghetto" and "urban blight" take on new meaning. No longer do you see Christian missionary work in the inner city as too costly for the small results, and begin backing those who do it.

Changes in family situations can force us to alter our moral stand. Christians were once horrified at the idea of organ transplants because those who performed them seemed to be playing God. Besides, some said, don't we need to stay intact so that our bodies, when resurrected, will be *ours?* Or perhaps we said that, since insurance often won't cover it, it's a luxury our nation simply can't afford, paying for all these transplants.

Now it's our niece who must have a kidney to survive — and the family insurance won't pay for it. So, prayerfully, we go back to Scripture to see if the case we've made on an issue really does align with scriptural principles.

Along the same line, a church office staff in my town had to change their procedure when a stranger came asking for financial help. "Too many people hit all the churches in town with the same story and take as much as they can get," the secretary told me. "So, for example, if a person asks for gas money to get them to a clinic in the neighboring city, I go with them to the station to tank up." At least for some, schemes and scams have made church personnel's former guileless openhanded policy impossible to maintain.

LOSING CONVICTIONS

If convictions can grow, mature, be refined, or shift, they can also atrophy, be mothballed, or abandoned. I do not refer here to ones we've set aside temporarily because they're of lesser importance and conflict with those of someone close to us.

Atrophy is "a wasting away . . . or the failure of an organ or part to grow or develop."[1] A gradual process, it may not be noticeable until we need a conviction to hold us up. Maybe we're invited out to a bar with the boss after work "to unwind" and we find ourselves without the moral muscle we need.

We *mothball* a conviction if it gets too restrictive or cumbersome to wear. *I need to spend after-hours with the boss if I expect to get ahead.* So we pack our "no bars for me" vow away. *I'll wear that moral stand, but not now. Next winter, maybe. After I get where I want to go.*

The conviction we *abandon* is the one we leave behind like a discarded pet when we move. It's too expensive to keep and, anyway, it no longer fits in with the person we have become and the life we've made for ourselves.

If a conviction is genuine, how can such things happen?

Crushing Experiences. The disfiguring accident, the premature death of a loved one that can cause a strong belief to intensify, can also work in the reverse. When one couple's child was killed by a drunk driver, they forgave him and witnessed to him about Jesus Christ.

Others, though, turn angrily away from that Christian way to be.

What makes the difference? Ask women who "were tortured and refused to be released," who "faced jeers and flogging . . . chained . . . stoned . . . were sawed in two . . . put to death by the sword. They went about in sheepskins and goatskins, destitute, persecuted and mistreated.

"These were all commended for their faith" (Heb. 11:35-39, italics mine).

They knew God intimately.

They trusted Him wholly.

Here's how my husband put it when he reflected on a particularly difficult testing period in his own life. "If we allow the experience to crush our faith, our convictions may be demolished as well. After a season, hopefully, we'll begin again."

Inattention to Spiritual Health. What we believe is based on what we know, not on what we knew. What we stand for now is based on what we can believe now. In order to believe now, our faith must be nourished.

When nourishment is withheld long enough, our convictions can be destroyed because the faith on which they're built is depleted, like the physical bodies of women I know. Because they suffered from eating disorders and seemed unable to take nourishment, they were growing weak and ill. As a matter of fact, left to themselves they could have literally starved themselves to death.

No sensible person expected these women to gobble down a steak dinner and smack their lips the first day of treatment. It takes time, a grasp of the unhealthy patterns that put them where they are, and a commitment to regain health. Their very desire for food was gone.

SYMPTOMS OF SPIRITUAL ANOREXIA

That can happen spiritually. When life crowds in on me and I find myself settling for a quick verse and prayer on my way into the day, like the anorexic, I notice symptoms. Resentment stirs easily in me. Desire to make the best moral choices has faded. Then I become ashamed. I look to God for answers and immediately, I know.

I come back by looking first at God's signature in the maple tree outside my kitchen window where squirrels play. In the newly opened white rose alongside the front path. At the sparrows pecking in the feeder.

I bring out my journal and record where I've been, what unhealthy patterns have interfered, where I am now, and where I want to go. I take time to reflect on the nature of God in Scripture and to talk with Him, child to Father. Good spiritual health habits are essential for the woman who will remain morally strong.

Trouble hits like hammer blows because Satan is the prince of this world and life is, therefore, not fair. We've had it. Not a drop of energy left to stand morally tall and strong. So we take the path of least resistance.

"I'm just plain tired. First Daddy died. Then Mama was diagnosed with Alzheimer's and it was up to me to decide what to do. Not long after that, I found myself out of a job because the company shut down the plant and moved overseas. By that time, I was too tired to even be angry because of the injustice of the decision."

How to meet these times?

—Sit quietly in the presence of God not once, but regularly. Think only about the fact that you *are* in the very presence of the Almighty Himself. Show Him your bone weariness. When you're ready, tell Him whatever you need to say. Ask Him to heal you on the inside. Count on the fact that He not only wants to do that, but He will do that.

—Tell someone mature enough to listen with understanding how it is with you. Let them share your burdens. Doing so takes initiative when you're exhausted and depressed—not something you have much of, probably. But doing so is also absolutely essential if you want to avoid a moral downhill slide.

To remain strong, we must keep growing spiritually. We all know people who haven't grown and what the shuddering results are. Often they are one-issue Christians. We shake our heads and groan that they are definitely in a rut.

A rut is a groove or furrow made as we trudge in the same way of thinking or walking. No need to look to left or right. But ruts are narrow and confining.

Rut Christians fail to see moral issues in the broad perspective. Stealing from someone's wallet is wrong, they know. But producing inferior products and selling them at hefty prices? Eugenia Price recommends to us *The Wider Place.*

Not all change means growth, but growth usually does mean change. Longtime friends of ours who've been Christians over twenty-five years experienced that a few summers ago. Serving overseas as short-term missionaries, they wrote back, "What have we learned over here? One of the big things is realizing how very much time and priority we spent on earthly things that were of no spiritual benefit." They prayed that they'd be able to effect changes in lifestyle back home as a result of their shift in perspective.

Ruts become wider places as growth pushes us out and up. "Change is always hard for the man who is in a rut. For he has scaled down his living to that which he can handle comfortably and welcomes no change—or challenge—that would lift him."[2]

"Let us leave the elementary teachings about Christ and go on to maturity" (Heb. 6:1).

1. *Webster's New World Dictionary, Second College Edition.*
2. C. Neil Strait, compiled by Lloyd Cory, *Quotable Quotations* (Wheaton, Ill.: Victor Books, 1985), p. 55.

A Woman of Integrity

TWELVE 🍎

F our children in four years of marriage, including a pair of twins. Three more children followed. On rainy days, she said, "[I] became so sick of the smells of 'sour everything' that [I] felt [I] would never care to eat again."[1]

That harried mother was Harriet Beecher Stowe. The marriage that she made probably wasn't her dream come true either. At least one biographer suggests that she may have wed intellectual Professor Calvin Stowe in 1836 out of sympathy because he'd lost his first wife.

Even before that, Harriet's life hadn't been idyllic. Her mother died when she was small and her minister father, Lyman Beecher, was extremely strict.

At forty, "When her sixth child, her particular favorite, died of cholera in 1849, she felt that at her child's grave she finally understood the lot of the Negro mother separated from her child, and she vowed to do some special service in the Negro's behalf."[2]

The Fugitive Slave Law of 1850 sent her into action. Here's what she wrote about that law: "Christian and humane people actually recommending the remanding of escaped fugitives into slavery as a duty binding on good citizens . . . Christians cannot know what slavery is: if they did, such a question could never be open for discussion."[3]

Out of strong convictions she wrote *Uncle Tom's Cabin* — a book that sold a record-breaking 300,000 copies the first year. The dramatic saga of Uncle Tom, a dedicated Christian who is ultimately beaten to death by Simon Legree, inflamed the passions of its readers and has been called one factor which led to the Civil War and the freeing of the slaves.

Stowe was harangued by those who opposed her book. "Many papers denounced her as a libeler of her country and as a sycophantic ally of the British redcoats. More of the same sort of abuse was. . . common and, as Mrs. Stowe knew, so unjustified."[4] She was convinced that her position as an abolitionist was right. That it was biblical.

After dramatizing the tragedy of slavery in story form, she concluded her book by reminding readers of the truth: that slaves were treated as property. That black people could not testify in court against a white. That there were no laws to protect a slave. So they could be sold separately; children could be taken from their parents.

"Both North and South have been guilty before God; and the *Christian Church* has a heavy account to answer," she wrote in the last paragraph of *Uncle Tom's Cabin*. "Not by combining together to protect injustice and cruelty and making a common capital of sin, is this Union to be saved — but by repentance, justice, and mercy."[5]

Harriet Beecher Stowe robs us of our excuses. *I don't have time. . . . I have too much on my mind already. . . . Let others take a stand on this. . . . Just let me live in peace.*

Like many issues we face today, slavery fit the category of nonabsolutes; there was no commandment against it in the Scripture; slavery was practiced in Bible times. North and South both defended their positions with chapter and verse.

STAND STRONG

Throughout history, women *have* stood strongly for what they believed was right. More of the stories in history books are of men, of course, because women have faced more obstacles in doing so—from the church and from society. *Thinking* was not their lot in life, they were told all too frequently, much less adopting a controversial ethic. Nevertheless, there have been others who have done just that.

Sister Blandina Segale ended the lynch law in Colorado. In 1878, the twenty-two-year-old traveled there alone, and for the next eighteen years was instrumental in building a school and hospital.

It happened the day a student told the sister, "Dad shot a man! He's in jail. A mob has gathered." The minute the victim died, they would lynch the boy's father.

Early the next morning, the sister convinced the sheriff to accompany her to the prisoner's cell, then walk with her and the prisoner past the mob to the bedside of the dying man, where the prisoner would ask for forgiveness.

The would-be lynchers silently stood aside and let them through. Victim forgave prisoner. "The law must take its course—not mob law," Sister stated firmly. Those standing outside that room heard. The prisoner was returned to his cell where he awaited trial.[6]

Frail Catherine Mumford Booth, cofounder with her husband William of the Salvation Army, was convinced that women were created to minister for God alongside men. She helped draw up the regulations that stated, "The Army refuses to make any difference between men and women as to rank, authority and duties."[7] Wife and mother Barbe Avrillot Acarie spearheaded the first private charitable works to the sick and poor of Paris. Later, after husband Jean-Pierre entered a monastery and she entered a convent, Madame Acarie introduced the Carmelite Order into France and was active in religious reformation.

When Lucy Webb Hayes became first lady in 1877, "Not everyone was thrilled by the new Wesleyan White House." Not only were there Sunday night hymn-singings but, with her husband's support, she set down a temperance policy. Detractors called her "Lemonade Lucy."[8]

Should we expect to change the course of world history by knowing our moral mind and standing by it? Maybe not, but we should expect to change our particular world.

Caroline did just that, even though she failed to persuade the legal system that she was right. It began when her teenage daughter objected to the book she'd been assigned to read by a substitute teacher because of what the girl considered to be vulgar and blasphemous language. The regular teacher, when she returned, apologized and assigned an alternate book.

Caroline requested the original book be removed from the required reading list. "I felt as though I had a responsibility." School officials refused. An attorney volunteered to represent her without charge. For five years, the case went through a series of lower court appeals and then finally to the Supreme Court, which refused to hear the case.

When Katie gave birth to a baby who had only a brain stem, she and her husband took the little girl home instead of leaving her in the hospital. The couple believed wholeheartedly that this baby was a person created in God's spiritual image. Despite emotional pain, they loved and cherished their child during her very brief life on earth.

Caroline was salt to people who followed the case in her city. Katie was light to the hospital staff, family, friends, and acquaintances. The situations that confront most of us may be less dramatic and touch a smaller group of people. But everyday morality is the kind that's needed most.

EVERYDAY MORALITY

—"You've undercharged me for the potatoes." Others in line hear.

—"I'm not going to claim those expenses on my taxes because they're not legitimate." Your tax-adviser friend looks quizzical.

—"I already promised to hire Bill to help paint the house and I won't change just because someone else says now that they'll do it cheaper." Your kids solemnly absorb what you've said.

—"We aren't going to watch that TV show. The guy who's supposed to be the hero knocks people around and asks questions later. But the barbeque's still hot; you can go out and roast marshmallows instead." Your daughter's friends store the incident away in their minds.

We're called to be morally decisive women. That's why God was saddened when I hid behind my husband—*You decide what's right and I'll go along.* I am a separate human being with my own moral nature. I know now that neither I nor any other woman is to hide behind submission and femininity like a Muslim behind her veil.

"We must train our faculties by practice to distinguish between good and evil," says Elisabeth Elliot.[9] When we accept that as our calling from God and commit ourselves to it—to know what's right for us and stand for that right—we are on our way to *becoming* women of integrity—or moral principle. "He called you to this through our gospel, that you might share in the glory of our Lord Jesus Christ. So then, [sisters], stand firm" (2 Thes. 2:14-15).

As we pursue the process outlined in this book, we'll be internalizing biblical principles. Those principles will work together to become the personal value system out of which we live—*our* value system.

Challenging ourselves to be that kind of woman can be postponed no longer. "The end of all things is near" (1 Peter 4:7).

Mankind's wickedness is filling the earth and every inclination of the thoughts of his heart is only evil all the time (Gen. 6:5).

He is a lover of himself and of money. He boasts of his discoveries and advances and that he is a master of his own destiny; he abuses others and leaves moaning, wounded victims behind; he is contemptuous toward parents; has never learned to love; is pleasure-bent; nods to God and goes his own way (2 Tim. 3:1-5).

We can't stop the end from coming. But we can, by living as a decisive woman, hold back the dragon and his evil ways in some corner of society. As we model an ethical lifestyle, we'll elevate Jesus Christ where He is being blasphemed or patronizingly tolerated now. As a result, some may even take a second, searching look and be moved closer toward falling in love with Him.

We must never underestimate our influence. As we've seen, it's mothers who make instant moral decisions about the tightness of jeans and sayings on T-shirts. Wives and singles often are the ones who decide what value system to employ with everyone from the paper boy to the city council.

It's not going to get easier to decide; it's going to get harder. Complex issues won't go away. As a matter of fact, they'll proliferate and at the same time, the influence of a deteriorating society will be more powerful.

Some of the questions with which we'll have to deal:

—Do only those who can pay get adequate health care?

—What guidelines shall be employed in treating unborn children in the womb?

—What moral standards will we apply to political figures?

—How aggressive should medical personnel be in caring for premature babies when survival statistics are very poor and prognosis for anything like a normal life if they do survive is extremely doubtful?

—What guidelines should be applied to the geneticist so that he or she uses that science for good instead of evil?

—The problems of nuclear and other waste and environmental pollution are growing more and more ugly. How shall we cope with them?

Thinking, deciding, and standing firm are hard work in the best of times. It's always going to be something we want to avoid—especially when our energy is depleted because life is pressing in on us from all sides. As pressure increases, the desire to escape will grow stronger.

That's one reason why we must move toward one another—Christian sister to Christian sister—in organized, small-group Bible studies and discussion groups or informal koinonia over tea in our living rooms. *Here's what I'm trying to decide. . . . Will you hold me accountable to study it through in the Bible before I act? Will you pray with me? Will you let me bounce my ideas off you? Will you let me do the same for you?*

To keep myself going into the wind, I have written a kind of personal manifesto in the back of my journal. I suggest that you write one of your own based on the following ideas:

I have been created in God's image as a female human being to be His representative on earth. *Be that woman.*

I have been equipped with a decision-making center to use

in deciding what's right, and a Book containing God's principles by which I am to make those decisions. *Use both of these.*

I am to cultivate my personal moral nature in order to grow into the likeness of Jesus Christ. Christ Himself is my example, so I'll take responsibility to study His life consistently. *Do that.*

I am not doing this alone. Father God aches to help me discover what the best choice is for me in a given situation. *Choose to count on Him.*

I will make wrong choices. It's not my flawless personal ethic that most pleases God (He knows it will never be flawless); it's my dedication to the process. *Keep reminding myself of that.*

I am to organize my life so I do have time and energy to think things through and decide. That is a priority. *Check regularly to see that I do so.*

I will not give equal importance to every issue. Some, like those that affect human life, have priority. Neither will I become a one-issue Christian—using all my passion on abortion or AIDS or pornography and dodging others that loom large in my life. *Work for balance.*

Set no grand goals. Be satisfied only to live gritty day by gritty day . . .

Loved by the Father
Dependent on the Son
Filled with the Spirit of Truth.

"To Him who is able to keep you from falling and to bring you faultless and joyful before His glorious presence—to the only God our Savior, through Jesus Christ our Lord, be glory, majesty, might, and authority, from all ages past, and now, and forever and ever! Amen" (Jude 24-25, GNB).

1. John R. Adams, *Harriet Beecher Stowe* (Boston: Twayne Publishing Company, 1963), p. 26.
2. *Encyclopaedia Britannica*, 1991, p. 776.

3. Harriet Beecher Stowe, *Uncle Tom's Cabin* (New York: The Mershon Co.), p. 498.
4. John R. Adams, *Harriet Beecher Stowe* (Boston: Twayne Publishing Company, 1963), p. 26.
5. Harriet Beecher Stowe, *Uncle Tom's Cabin* (New York: The Mershon Co.), p. 505.
6. Rosemary Rodford Ruether and Rosemary Skinner Keller, *Women and Religion in America*, Vol. 1 (San Francisco: Harper and Row Publishers, 1981), pp. 141–44.
7. Susan Raven and Alison Weir, *Women of Achievement* (New York: Harmony Books, 1981), p. 97.
8. Paul F. Boller, Jr., *Presidential Wives* (New York: Oxford University Press, 1988), p. 148.
9. Elisabeth Elliot, *The Liberty of Obedience* (Waco, Texas: Word Books, 1969), p. 57.

Questions

CHAPTER ONE

1. If you were talking with a retreat leader, what moral dilemma would you ask about?
2. How would you advise the mother whose son is homosexual? The wife of the abusive husband? The mother of the abusive daughter?
3. What are some of the moral values you were taught growing up? Are they still part of your value system?
4. Review the four reasons it's hard to make moral choices. Which reason has affected you most?
5. List various roles of your life like job, homemaker, club member, citizen. In which do you have the most difficulty making these choices and why?
6. Reread Psalm 32:8 and John 16:13 at the end of this chapter. List the four italicized words. How do they encourage you in your quest to be a decisive woman?

CHAPTER TWO

1. Review your own growing up years to see who your au-

thority figures were. How ready were you to think for
yourself as an adult? What effect has that had on you?

2. Which of the specific reasons listed hit home and why?

3. In your own words, paraphrase the definition of "ethics" and "morals."

4. Which do you have more of: convictions, preferences,
or opinions? Give an example of each.

5. Think of a modern situation parallel to either Esther or
Ruth and imagine yourself as the main character. What
are your thoughts as you try to make the decision? Your
feelings?

6. Do you agree that women have a biblical responsibility
to make personal moral choices? Support your stand
using scriptural evidence in this chapter.

CHAPTER THREE

1. Read the Ten Commandments in Exodus 20 and think
of ways that you use at least five of them as guidelines
in your daily life.

2. Based on your convictions, what do you think you
might have done if you were Lynda?

3. Come up with one way not mentioned in chapter 3 that
each of the New Testament directives mentioned apply
(Matt. 6:19; Mark 12:17; 1 Cor. 6:20; Heb. 12:16;
James 2:1).

4. Many rights are guaranteed citizens based on the principle that "All men are created equal." Name several
that are important to you.

5. Imagine you were explaining to a friend why God didn't
give us commandments to cover every moral choice
but provided principles instead. What would you say?

6. Write a journal entry in your own words based on a par-

able, psalm, or proverb not mentioned in this chapter that addresses right and wrong.

CHAPTER FOUR

1. Even though she is a sinner, a Christian woman can use her mind to think through a moral choice. Why? What Scripture supports your stand?
2. Evaluate the kind of conscience you have — from overscrupulous to inactive. What experiences have contributed to its state? How does God mean you to improve its trustworthiness?
3. Describe your emotional makeup. How has it helped or hindered the decisions you've made? Read Matthew 9:36 and John 15:32 and reflect on how Jesus' examples apply to you.
4. When it comes to making decisions, do you identify more with Jean or Evie? To use this faculty most effectively, what changes do you need to let God help you make?
5. Restate 1 Corinthians 2:11-12 and John 16:11 so they apply directly to you. Substitute personal pronouns. What are some ways you can cultivate the ability to hear God's silent inner voice?
6. Describe the decision-making center God has given you. What new thoughts about making moral choices do you have?

CHAPTER FIVE

1. Think of one of the hardest moral choices you've ever had to make. What process did you use to decide?

2. What person has impressed you because he or she has stood for a particular conviction and as a result was salt and light? What has knowing that person done for you?
3. Reread the Golden Rule and use it to decide what to do in the following situations:
     A neighbor ignores you
     A coworker asks you to cover for her by saying she was sick when she was not
4. In what ways has Christ made you free? How does the statement that if a thing is not commanded or forbidden in the Bible, you have liberty to decide what to do, make you feel? Think of three areas where this applies.
5. Read Romans 14:1–15:4. Jot down statements that provide guidance in making moral choices. Show how they apply to one situation in your life.
6. In what ways do you think the principle of love is most misunderstood? Do you agree or disagree that Dodie applied the principle of love correctly? Why or why not?

CHAPTER SIX

1. When faced with a moral decision, how do you normally resolve it? In what ways is the process you use effective? Ineffective?
2. Practice finding out what a passage means by choosing a psalm, looking up words of which you are uncertain, and reading it in a couple of other translations.
3. How do the verses before and after 1 Corinthians 9:6 contribute to its meaning?
4. What cultural situations are described in John 2?
5. Choose the principle based either on the Twenty-Third Psalm, the Parable of the Good Samaritan, or the

Love Chapter and come up with a way you could apply it to a moral dilemma you have faced or are facing now.

6. During your regular Bible study this week, find at least one passage on which you can base a biblical principle and do so.

CHAPTER SEVEN

1. Number a list of moral dilemmas about which you need convictions, making the one you want to decide about first number one, the next two, etc.
2. Be sure that you don't have unforgiven sin and then use Ephesians 1:17-19 as a format for prayer.
3. Choose the number-one dilemma and write down the specific questions to which you need to find an answer. Then write down the moral issues it brings to mind. Brainstorm your thoughts on the subject.
4. Choose key words to look up in the subject index of a Bible and list passages that apply.
5. Do any of the five principles in chapter 5 apply? If so, how?
6. Summarize the biblical teachings and write out a principle or principles based on the summary or summaries.

CHAPTER EIGHT

1. Write a few sentences or paragraphs telling how the principles you formed in chapter 7 apply to your particular situation.
2. Now write a statement of conclusion like the ones on money or infertility in this chapter.
3. Look for a book or magazine article that provides addi-

tional information and note important points.

4. Talk with a mature Christian friend about the issue. Write down and reflect on any new perspectives you receive.

5. While you're giving all the information time to incubate, reflect on Philip Yancey's statement that God "commands us to do slowly and blunderingly what He could do perfectly and in the twinkling of an eye."

6. If you'd been a friend of Dale's, what might you have said to him during a visit before the hospital personnel pulled the plug?

CHAPTER NINE

1. Read Luke 14:28-31 and look for phrases that describe actions you might have to take to stand by a conviction.

2. Go over the list of things that living by a conviction has cost people. Which would be hardest for you? Which next hardest? Look at Exodus 15:2; Matthew 28:20; and Acts 1:8 and in your own words write promises on which you can count.

3. Which of the following will you do to express your conviction about an issue? Write a letter to the editor of a newspaper, make a contribution of time, money, or goods to a cause supporting that issue, or promise yourself to state your point of view in love when the occasion arises.

4. What's been your reaction when you've failed to live by a conviction? What's one thing you can do so failure can become your teacher?

5. Review some important convictions and the potential price tag each might have. Read Ephesians 1:19-20 and

reflect on your resources.

6. What biblical principles would you consider if you had to make a decision like Darcie's? Could a Christian woman in Darcie's position make another choice and feel biblically justified?

CHAPTER TEN

1. Rate yourself:
   I avoid conflict at all cost
   I dislike conflict but will confront if necessary
   I love a good argument
2. What recreational practices cause the most differences of opinion in your life? What impact have these situations had?
3. What are the main reasons you have conflicts about moral choices with those close to you?
4. Think of a scenario in which such a conflict is taking place. What could you do to promote better communication?
5. If you're married, put into practice the attitude of Ephesians 4:2 next time a conflict arises. If you're single, do so in a close relationship. Record what happens and draw conclusions.
6. On what subjects are you willing to compromise? Why? Do you think it's acceptable to choose the greatest good? Under what circumstances? In what ways does Ephesians 4:3, 13 speak to you?

CHAPTER ELEVEN

1. Read the complete account of Peter's vision in Acts 10

and put yourself in Peter's place, feeling what he must have felt. Why was this change in conviction one of the most important experiences of his life?

2. Is change hard for you? Do you tend to cling to old ideas because they're safe or are you open to new ones? If you've changed in a value, think back as to how it came about.

3. Have you had a new experience that's shown you a new slant on a particular issue? What have you learned?

4. Reflect on atrophied convictions, mothballed convictions, and abandoned convictions in your own life. Decide the steps you must take if you are in a decline.

5. Why is it dangerous to become a one-issue Christian?

6. What positive changes in forming a value system do you need to aim for? How does Hebrews 6:1 apply?

CHAPTER TWELVE

1. What message do the stories of Harriet Beecher Stowe, Blandina Segale, Catherine Booth, Barbe Acarie, and Lucy Hayes leave with you?

2. In what areas do you have an influence because of your moral choices? Think of reasons why your influence is important.

3. Why is it urgent that you become a decisive woman now? See 1 Peter 4:7.

4. Think of yourself as a woman of integrity. What does that mean to you? Are your ideas realistic and achievable?

5. How can your church help you formulate a personal value system? Talk over your ideas with a member of your church staff.

6. Write a personal manifesto based on the ideas at the

end of chapter 12. Keep them where you'll review them
often. What encouraging promises does God make in
Jude 24-25?